MATLAB Linear Algebra

César Pérez López

Apress®

MATLAB Linear Algebra

ISBN-13 (pbk): 978-1-4842-0323-1

ISBN-13 (electronic): 978-1-4842-0322-4

Publisher: Heinz Weinheimer
Lead Editor: Dominic Shakeshaft
Editorial Board: Steve Anglin, Mark Beckner, Ewan Buckingham, Gary Cornell, Louise Corrigan, Jim DeWolf,
    Jonathan Gennick, Robert Hutchinson, Michelle Lowman, James Markham, Matthew Moodie,
    Jeff Olson, Jeffrey Pepper, Douglas Pundick, Ben Renow-Clarke, Dominic Shakeshaft, Gwenan Spearing,
    Matt Wade, Steve Weiss
Coordinating Editor: Jill Balzano
Copy Editor: Barnaby Sheppard
Compositor: SPi Global
Indexer: SPi Global
Artist: SPi Global
Cover Designer: Anna Ishchenko

Distributed to the book trade worldwide by Springer Science+Business Media New York, 233 Spring Street, 6th Floor, New York, NY 10013. Phone 1-800-SPRINGER, fax (201) 348-4505, e-mail orders-ny@springer-sbm.com, or visit www.springeronline.com. Apress Media, LLC is a California LLC and the sole member (owner) is Springer Science + Business Media Finance Inc (SSBM Finance Inc). SSBM Finance Inc is a Delaware corporation.

For information on translations, please e-mail rights@apress.com, or visit www.apress.com.

Apress and friends of ED books may be purchased in bulk for academic, corporate, or promotional use. eBook versions and licenses are also available for most titles. For more information, reference our Special Bulk Sales–eBook Licensing web page at www.apress.com/bulk-sales.

Any source code or other supplementary material referenced by the author in this text is available to readers at www.apress.com. For detailed information about how to locate your book's source code, go to www.apress.com/source-code/.

Contents at a Glance

Contents

About the Author

César Pérez López is a Professor at the Department of Statistics and Operations Research at the University of Madrid. César is also a Mathematician and Economist at the National Statistics Institute (INE) in Madrid, a body which belongs to the Superior Systems and Information Technology Department of the Spanish Government. César also currently works at the Institute for Fiscal Studies in Madrid.

Coming Soon

- *MATLAB Programming for Numerical Analysis,* 978-1-4842-0296-8
- *MATLAB Differential Equations,* 978-1-4842-0311-8
- *MATLAB Control Systems Engineering,* 978-1-4842-0290-6
- *MATLAB Differential and Integral Calculus,* 978-1-4842-0305-7
- *MATLAB Matrix Algebra,* 978-1-4842-0308-8

CHAPTER 1

■ ■ ■

MATLAB Introduction and Working Environment

The MATLAB Working Environment

The following table summarizes the main components of the MATLAB working environment.

Tool	Description
Command History	This presents a history of the functions introduced in the Command Window and allows you to copy and execute them (see the lower right part of Figure 1-2).
Command Window	This is the window in which you execute MATLAB commands (see the central part of Figure 1-2).
Workspace	This shows the present contents of the workspace and allows you to make changes to it (see the upper right part of Figure 1-2).
Help	This allows you to search and read the documentation for the complete family of MATLAB products.
Start button	This runs tools and gives you access to documentation for all MathWorks products currently installed on your computer (Figure 1-3).

Figure 1-1 shows the screen in which you enter MATLAB programs. This is MATLAB's primary work environment.

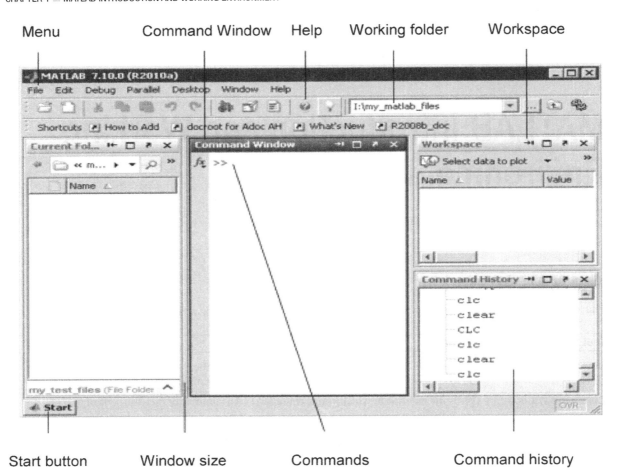

Menu   Command Window   Help   Working folder   Workspace

Start button   Window size   Commands   Command history

Figure 1-1.

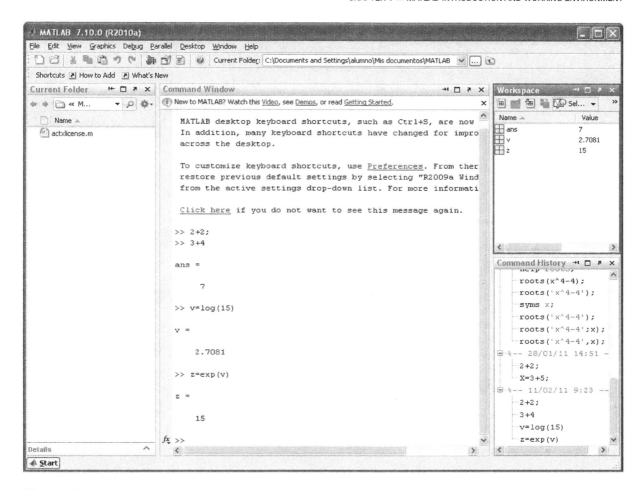

Figure 1-2.

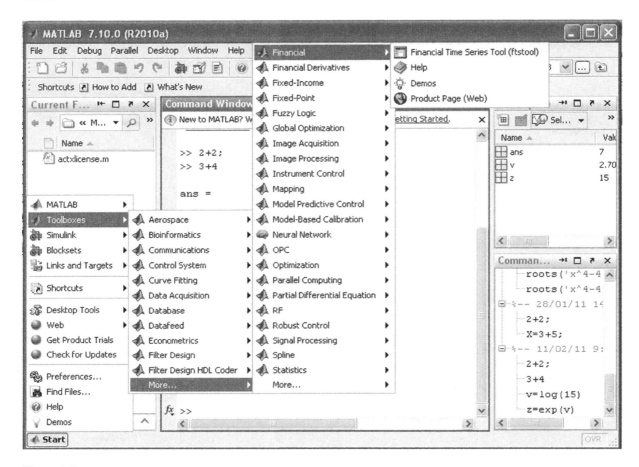

Figure 1-3.

Any MATLAB commands are entered in the Command Window to the right of the user input prompt ">>" and the response will appear in the lines immediately below, after pressing *Enter*. After the command has been executed the user input prompt will reappear, allowing you to enter more commands (Figure 1-4).

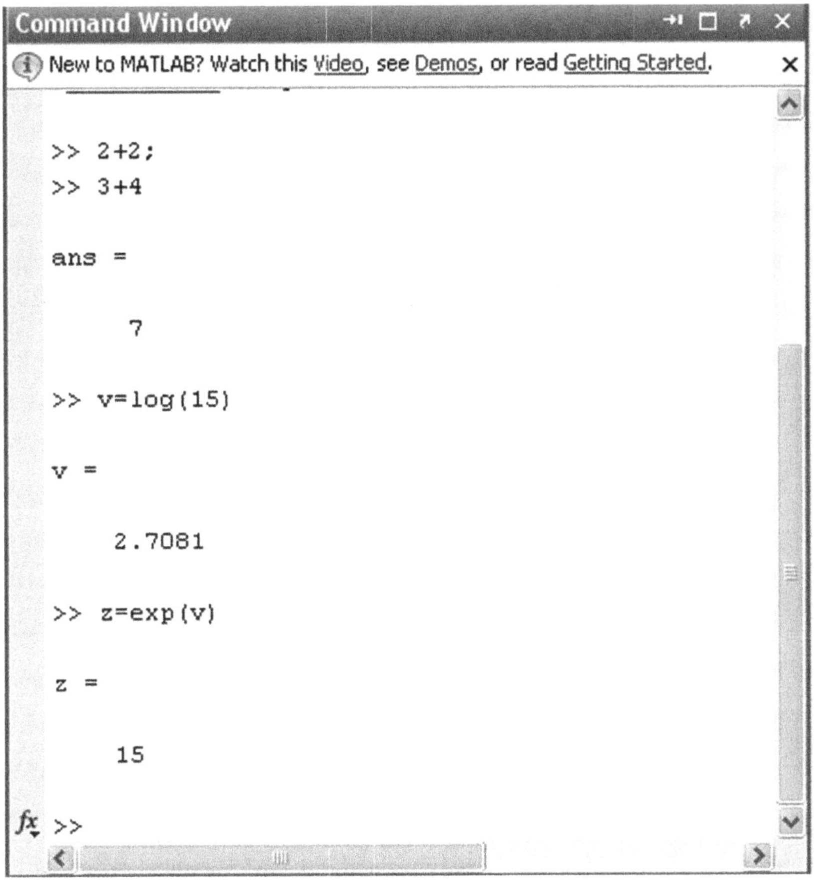

Command Window

ⓘ New to MATLAB? Watch this Video, see Demos, or read Getting Started.

```
>> 2+2;
>> 3+4

ans =

    7

>> v=log(15)

v =

    2.7081

>> z=exp(v)

z =

    15

fx >>
```

Figure 1-4.

If the result of a command is not assigned to a variable, MATLAB will return the response using the expression *ans* =, as shown at the beginning of Figure 1-4. If the result is assigned to a variable then we can use that variable as an argument in subsequent commands. This is the case for the variable v in Figure 1-4, which is subsequently used as input for an exponential.

To execute a MATLAB command, simply press *Enter* once the command is written. If at the end of the input we put a semicolon, the program will execute the command and keep the result in memory (*Workspace*), but it will not display the result on screen (see the first input in Figure 1-13). The input prompt ">>" will then reappear to indicate that you can enter a new command.

Like the C programming language, MATLAB is case sensitive; for example, $Sin(x)$ is not the same as $sin(x)$. The names of all built-in functions begin with a lowercase character. There should be no spaces in the names of commands, variables or functions. In other cases, spaces are ignored, and they can be used to make the input more readable. Multiple entries can be entered in the same command line by separating them with commas, pressing *Enter* at the end of the last entry (see Figure 1-4). If you use a semicolon at the end of one of the entries in the line, its corresponding output will not be displayed.

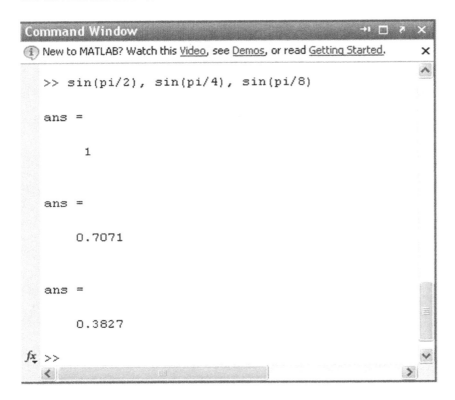

Figure 1-5.

Descriptive comments can be entered in a command input line by starting them with the "%" symbol. When you run the input, MATLAB ignores the comment and processes the rest of the code (see Figure 1-6).

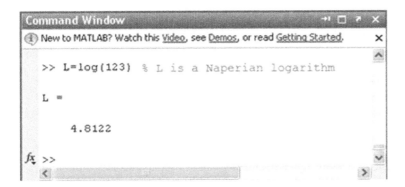

Figure 1-6.

To simplify the process of entering script to be evaluated by the MATLAB interpreter (via the Command Window prompt), you can use the arrow keys. For example, if you press the up arrow key once, you will recover the last entry you submitted. If you press the up key twice, you will recover the penultimate entry you submitted, and so on.

If you type a sequence of characters in the input area and then press the up arrow key, you will recover the last entry you submitted that begins with the specified string.

Commands entered during a MATLAB session are temporarily stored in the buffer (*Workspace*) until you end the session, at which time they can be permanently stored in a file or are permanently lost.

Below is a summary of the keys that can be used in MATLAB's input area (command line), together with their functions:

Up arrow (Ctrl-P)	Retrieves the previous entry.
Down arrow (Ctrl-N)	Retrieves the following entry.
Left arrow (Ctrl-B)	Moves the cursor one character to the left.
Right arrow (Ctrl-F)	Moves the cursor one character to the right.
CTRL-left arrow	Moves the cursor one word to the left.
CTRL-right arrow	Moves the cursor one word to the right.
Home (Ctrl-A)	Moves the cursor to the beginning of the line.
End (Ctrl-E)	Moves the cursor to the end of the current line.
Escape	Clears the command line.
Delete (Ctrl-D)	Deletes the character indicated by the cursor.
Backspace	Deletes the character to the left of the cursor.
CTRL-K	Deletes (kills) the current line.

The command *clc* clears the command window, but does not delete the contents of the work area (the contents remain in the memory).

Help in MATLAB

You can find help for MATLAB via the help button ⓘ in the toolbar or via the *Help* option in the menu bar. In addition, support can also be obtained via MATLAB commands. The command *help* provides general help on all MATLAB commands (see Figure 1-7). By clicking on any of them, you can get more specific help. For example, if you click on *graph2d*, you get support for two-dimensional graphics (see Figure 1-8).

Figure 1-7.

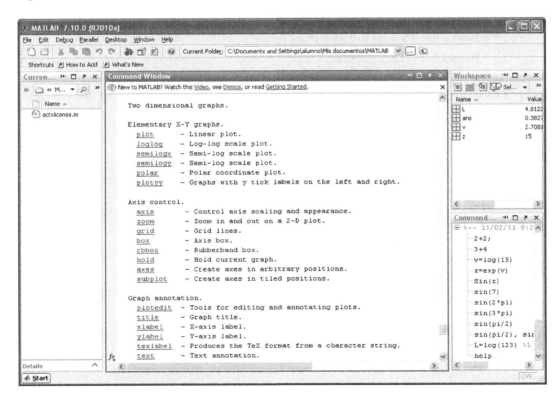

Figure 1-8.

You can ask for help about a specific command *command* (Figure 1-9) or on any topic *topic* (Figure 1-10) by using the command *help command* or *help topic*.

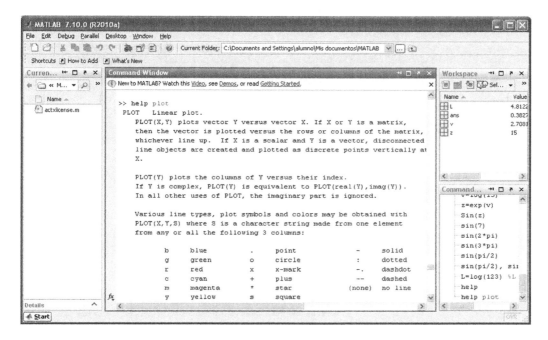

Figure 1-9.

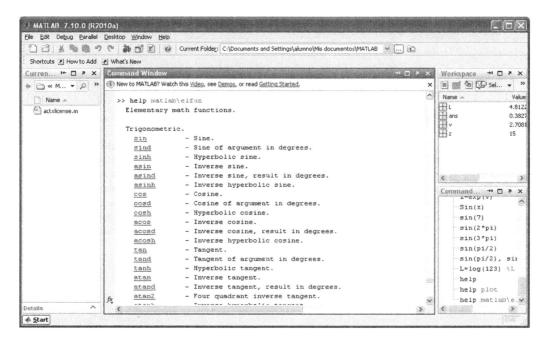

Figure 1-10.

The command *lookfor string* allows you to find all those MATLAB functions or commands that refer to or contain the string *string*. This command is very useful when there is no direct support for the specified string, or to view the help for all commands related to the given string. For example, if we want to find help for all commands that contain the sequence *inv*, we can use the command *lookfor inv* (Figure 1-11).

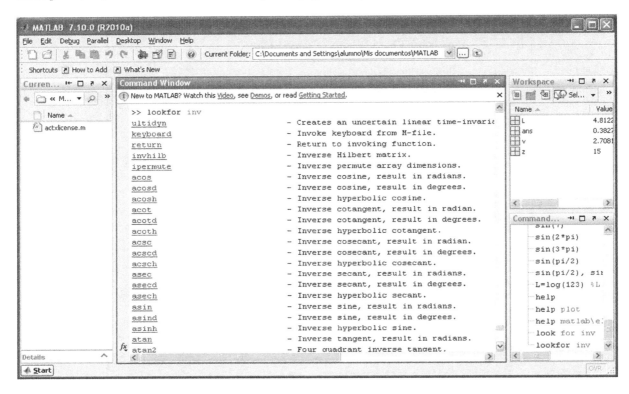

Figure 1-11.

Numerical Computation with MATLAB

You can use MATLAB as a powerful numerical computer. While most calculators handle numbers only to a preset degree of precision, MATLAB performs exact calculations to any desired degree of precision. In addition, unlike calculators, we can perform operations not only with individual numbers, but also with objects such as arrays.

Most of the topics of classical numerical analysis are treated by this software. It supports matrix calculus, statistics, interpolation, least squares fitting, numerical integration, minimization of functions, linear programming, numerical and algebraic solutions of differential equations and a long list of further methods that we'll meet as this book progresses.

Here are some examples of numerical calculations with MATLAB. (As we know, to obtain the results it is necessary to press *Enter* once the desired command has been entered after the prompt ">>".)

We simply calculate 4 + 3 to obtain the result 7. To do this, just type 4 + 3, and then *Enter*.

>> *4 + 3*

ans =

7

We find the value of 3 to the power of 100, without having previously set the precision. To do this we simply enter 3 ^ 100.

>> **3 ^ 100**

ans =

5. 1538e + 047

We can use the command "format long e" to obtain results to 15 digits (floating-point).

>> **format long e**

>> **3^100**

ans =

5.153775207320115e+047

We can also work with complex numbers. We find the result of the operation raising $(2 + 3i)$ to the power 10 by typing the expression $(2 + 3i) ^ 10$.

>> **(2 + 3i) ^ 10**

ans =

-1 415249999999998e + 005 - 1. 456680000000000e + 005i

The previous result is also available in short format, using the "format short" command.

>> **format short**
>> **(2 + 3i)^10**

ans =

-1.4152e+005- 1.4567e+005i

We can calculate the value of the Bessel function J_0 at 11.5. To do this we type besselj(0,11.5).

>> *besselj(0,11.5)*

ans =

   -0.0677

Symbolic Calculations with MATLAB

MATLAB perfectly handles symbolic mathematical computations, manipulating and performing operations on formulae and algebraic expressions with ease. You can expand, factor and simplify polynomials and rational and trigonometric expressions, find algebraic solutions of polynomial equations and systems of equations, evaluate derivatives and integrals symbolically, find solutions of differential equations, manipulate powers, and investigate limits and many other features of algebraic series.

To perform these tasks, MATLAB first requires all the variables (or algebraic expressions) to be written between single quotes. When MATLAB receives a variable or expression in quotes, it is interpreted as symbolic.

Here are some examples of symbolic computations with MATLAB.

1. We can expand the following algebraic expression: $((x+1)(x+2) - (x+2)^2)^3$. This is done by typing: expand('((x+1)(x+2) - (x+2)^2)^3'). The result will be another algebraic expression:

    >> syms x; expand(((x + 1) *(x + 2)-(x + 2) ^ 2) ^ 3)

    ans =

    -x ^ 3-6 * x ^ 2-12 * x-8

2. We can factor the result of the calculation in the above example by typing: factor('((x+1) * (x+2) - (x+2)^2)^3')

    >> syms x; factor(((x + 1)*(x + 2)-(x + 2)^2)^3)

    ans =

    -(x + 2)^3

3. We can find the indefinite integral of the function $(x^2) \sin(x)^2$ by typing: int('x^2 *sin(x)^ 2', 'x')

    >> int('x^2*sin(x)^2', 'x')

    ans =

    x ^ 2 *(-1/2 * cos(x) * sin(x) + 1/2 * x)-1/2 * x * cos(x) ^ 2 + 1/4 * cos(x) * sin(x) + 1/4 * 1/x-3 * x ^ 3

4. We can simplify the previous result:

    >> syms x; simplify(int(x^2*sin(x)^2, x))

    ans =

    sin(2*x)/8 -(x*cos(2*x))/4 -(x^2*sin(2*x))/4 + x^3/6

5. We can present the previous result using a more elegant mathematical notation:

    >> syms x; pretty(simplify(int(x^2*sin(x)^2, x)))

    ans =

$$\frac{\sin(2x)}{8} - \frac{x \cos(2x)}{4} - \frac{x^2 \sin(2x)}{4} + \frac{x^3}{6}$$

6. We can solve the equation $3ax - 7 x^2 + x^3 = 0$ (where a is a parameter):

>> **solve('3*a*x-7*x^2 + x^3 = 0', 'x')**

ans =

```
[                          0]
[7/2 + 1/2 *(49-12*a) ^(1/2)]
[7/2-1/2 *(49-12*a) ^(1/2)]
```

On the other hand, MATLAB can use the Maple program libraries to work with symbolic math, and can thus extend its field of action. In this way, MATLAB can be used to work on such topics as differential forms, Euclidean geometry, projective geometry, statistics, etc.

At the same time, Maple can also benefit from MATLAB's powers of numerical calculation, which might be used, for example, in combination with the Maple libraries (combinatorics, optimization, number theory, etc.)

Graphics with MATLAB

MATLAB can generate two- and three-dimensional graphs, as well as contour and density plots. You can graphically represent data lists, controlling colors, shading and other graphics features. Animated graphics are also supported. Graphics produced by MATLAB are portable to other programs.

Some examples of MATLAB graphics are given below.

1. We can represent the function $x\sin(1/x)$ for x ranging between $-\pi/4$ and $\pi/4$, taking 300 equidistant points in the interval. See Figure 1-12.

```
>> x = linspace(-pi/4,pi/4,300);
>> y = x.*sin(1./x);
>> plot(x,y)
```

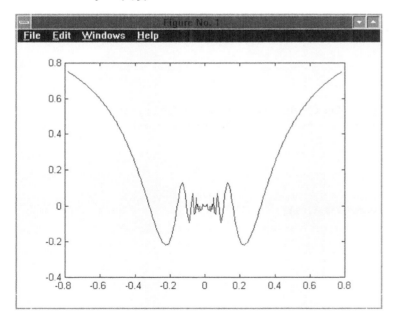

Figure 1-12.

2. We can give the above graph a title and label the axes, and we can add a grid. See Figure 1-13.

```
>> x = linspace(-pi/4,pi/4,300);
>> y = x.*sin(1./x);
>> plot(x,y);
>> grid;
>> xlabel('Independent variable X');
>> ylabel('Dependent variable Y');
>> title('The function y=xsin(1/x)')
```

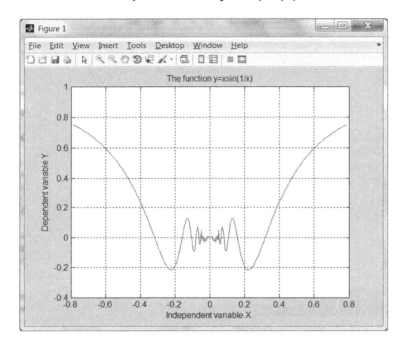

Figure 1-13.

3. We can generate a graph of the surface defined by the function $z = \sin(\mathrm{sqrt}(x^2 + y^2)) / \mathrm{sqrt}(x^2 + y^2)$, where x and y vary over the interval (-7.5, 7.5), taking equally spaced points 0.5 apart. See Figure 1-14.

```
>> x = -7.5:. 5:7.5;
>> y = x;
>> [X, Y] = meshgrid(x,y);
>> Z = sin(sqrt(X.^2+Y.^2))./sqrt(X.^2+Y.^2);
>> surf(X, Y, Z)
```

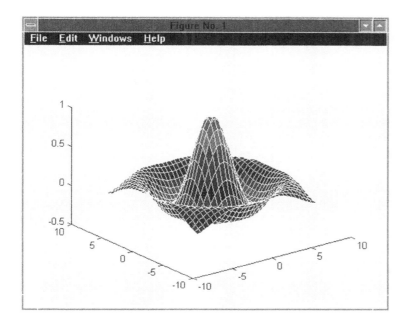

Figure 1-14.

These 3D graphics allow you to get a clear picture of figures in space, and are very helpful in visually identifying intersections between different bodies, and in generating all kinds of space curves, surfaces and volumes of revolution.

4.   We can generate the three dimensional graph corresponding to the helix with parametric coordinates: $x = \sin(t)$, $y = \cos(t)$, $z = t$. See Figure 1-15.

```
>> t = 0:pi/50:10*pi;
>> plot3(sin(t),cos(t),t)
```

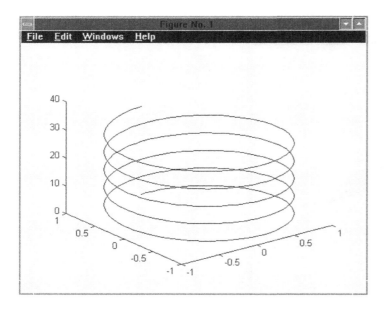

Figure 1-15.

5. We can represent a planar curve given by its polar coordinates r = cos(2*t*) * sin(2*t*) for *t* varying in the range between 0 and π by equally spaced points 0.01 apart. See Figure 1-16.

```
>> t = 0:. 1:2 * pi;
>> r = sin(2*t). * cos(2*t);
>> polar(t,r)
```

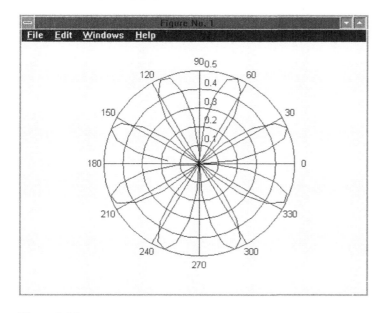

Figure 1-16.

6. We can make a graph of a symbolic function using the command "ezplot". See Figure 1-17.

```
>> y = 'x^3/(x^2-1)';
>> ezplot(y,[-5,5])
```

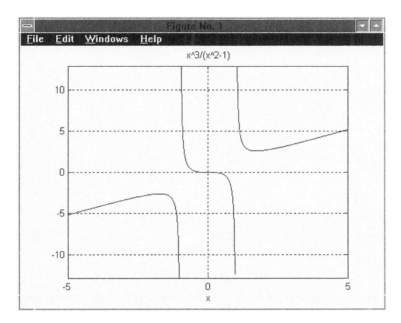

Figure 1-17.

We will go into these concepts in more detail in the chapter on graphics.

General Notation

As for any program, the best way to learn MATLAB is to use it. By practicing on examples you become familiar with the syntax and notation peculiar to MATLAB. Each example we give consists of the header with the user input prompt ">>" followed by the MATLAB response on the next line. See Figure 1-18.

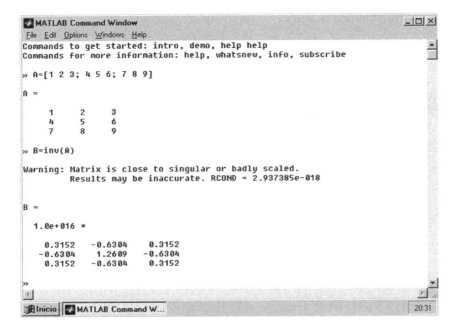

Figure 1-18.

At other times, depending on the type of entry (user input) given to MATLAB, the response is returned using the expression "ans =". See Figure 1-19.

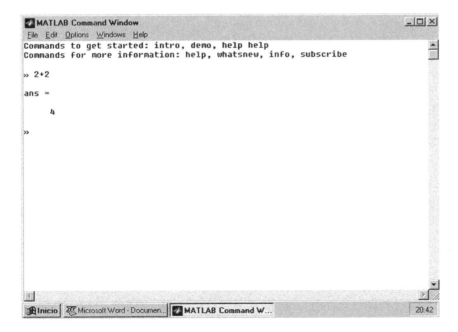

Figure 1-19.

It is important to pay attention to the use of uppercase versus lowercase letters, parentheses versus square brackets, spaces and punctuation (particularly commas and semicolons).

Help with Commands

We have already seen how you can get help using MATLAB's drop down menus.

But, in addition, support can also be obtained via commands (instructions or functions), implemented as MATLAB objects.

You can use the help command to get immediate access to diverse information.

>> *help*

```
HELP topics:

matlab\general    -  General purpose commands.
matlab\ops        -  Operators and special characters.
matlab\lang       -  Programming language constructs.
matlab\elmat      -  Elementary matrices and matrix manipulation.
matlab\elfun      -  Elementary math functions.
matlab\specfun    -  Specialized math functions.
matlab\matfun     -  Matrix functions - numerical linear algebra.
matlab\datafun    -  Data analysis and Fourier transforms.
matlab\polyfun    -  Interpolation and polynomials.
matlab\funfun     -  Function functions and ODE solvers.
matlab\sparfun    -  Sparse matrices.
matlab\graph2d    -  Two dimensional graphs.
matlab\graph3d    -  Three dimensional graphs.
matlab\specgraph  -  Specialized graphs.
matlab\graphics   -  Handle Graphics.
matlab\uitools    -  Graphical user interface tools.
matlab\strfun     -  Character strings.
matlab\iofun      -  File input/output.
matlab\timefun    -  Time and dates.
matlab\datatypes  -  Data types and structures.
matlab\winfun     -  Windows Operating System Interface Files(DDE/ActiveX)
matlab\demos      -  Examples and demonstrations.
toolbox\symbolic  -  Symbolic Math Toolbox.
toolbox\tour      -  MATLAB Tour
toolbox\local     -  Preferences.

For more help on directory/topic, type "help topic".
```

As we can see, the help command displays a list of program directories and their contents. Help on any given topic *topic* can be displayed using the command *help topic*. For example:

>> *help inv*

```
INV    Matrix inverse.
INV(X) is the inverse of the square matrix X.
A warning message is printed if X is badly scaled or
nearly singular.
```

See also SLASH, PINV, COND, CONDEST, NNLS, LSCOV.

Overloaded methods
help sym/inv.m

>> help matlab\elfun

Elementary math functions.

Trigonometric.

```
sin        - Sine.
sinh       - Hyperbolic sine.
asin       - Inverse sine.
asinh      - Inverse hyperbolic sine.
cos        - Cosine.
cosh       - Hyperbolic cosine.
acos       - Inverse cosine.
acosh      - Inverse hyperbolic cosine.
tan        - Tangent.
tanh       - Hyperbolic tangent.
atan       - Inverse tangent.
atan2      - Four quadrant inverse tangent.
atanh      - Inverse hyperbolic tangent.
sec        - Secant.
sech       - Hyperbolic secant.
asec       - Inverse secant.
asech      - Inverse hyperbolic secant.
csc        - Cosecant.
csch       - Hyperbolic cosecant.
acsc       - Inverse cosecant.
acsch      - Inverse hyperbolic cosecant.
cot        - Cotangent.
coth       - Hyperbolic cotangent.
acot       - Inverse cotangent.
acoth      - Inverse hyperbolic cotangent.
```

Exponential.

```
exp        - Exponential.
log        - Natural logarithm.
log10      - Common(base 10) logarithm.
log2       - Base 2 logarithm and dissect floating point number.
pow2       - Base 2 power and scale floating point number.
sqrt       - Square root.
nextpow2   - Next higher power of 2.
```

Complex.
```
abs        - Absolute value.
angle      - Phase angle.
conj       - Complex conjugate.
```

```
imag      - Complex imaginary part.
real      - Complex real part.
unwrap    - Unwrap phase angle.
isreal    - True for real array.
cplxpair  - Sort numbers into complex conjugate pairs.
```

Rounding and remainder.

```
fix       - Round towards zero.
floor     - Round towards minus infinity.
ceil      - Round towards plus infinity.
round     - Round towards nearest integer.
mod       - Modulus(signed remainder after division).
rem       - Remainder after division.
sign      - Signum.
```

There is a command for help on a certain sequence of characters (*lookfor string*) which allows you to find all those functions or commands that contain or refer to the given string *string*. This command is very useful when there is no direct support for the specified string, or if you want to view the help for all commands related to the given sequence. For example, if we seek help for all commands that contain the sequence *complex*, we can use the *lookfor complex* command to see which commands MATLAB provides.

>> lookfor complex

```
ctranspose.m: %'   Complex conjugate transpose.
CONJ    Complex conjugate.
CPLXPAIR Sort numbers into complex conjugate pairs.
IMAG    Complex imaginary part.
REAL    Complex real part.
CDF2RDF Complex diagonal form to real block diagonal form.
RSF2CSF Real block diagonal form to complex diagonal form.
B5ODE   Stiff problem, linear with complex eigenvalues(B5 of EHL).
CPLXDEMO Maps of functions of a complex variable.
CPLXGRID Polar coordinate complex grid.
CPLXMAP Plot a function of a complex variable.
GRAFCPLX Demonstrates complex function plots in MATLAB.
ctranspose.m: %TRANSPOSE Symbolic matrix complex conjugate transpose.
SMOKE   Complex matrix with a "smoke ring" pseudospectrum.
```

MATLAB and Programming

By properly combining all the objects defined in MATLAB, according to the rules of syntax of the program, you can build useful mathematical programming code. Programs usually consist of a series of instructions in which values are calculated, are assigned names and are reused in further calculations.

As in programming languages like C or FORTRAN, in MATLAB you can write programs with loops, control flow and conditionals. MATLAB can write procedural programs, i.e., it can define a sequence of standard steps to run. As in C or Pascal, a Do, For, or While loop can be used for repetitive calculations. The language of MATLAB also includes conditional constructs such as If--Then--Else. MATLAB also supports different logical operators, such as AND, OR, NOT and XOR.

MATLAB supports procedural programming (with iterative processes, recursive functions, loops, etc.), functional programming and object-oriented programming. Here are two simple examples of programs. The first generates the Hilbert matrix of order n, and the second calculates all the Fibonacci numbers less than 1000.

```
% Generating the Hilbert matrix of order n
t = '1/(i+j-1)';
for i = 1:n
for j = 1:n
a(i,j) = eval(t);
end
end

% Calculating the Fibonacci numbers
f = [1 1]; i = 1;
while f(i) + f(i-1) < 1000
f(i+2) = f(i) + f(i+1);
i = i+1
end
```

Commands to Exit and Escape to the MS-DOS Environment

There are three ways you can escape from the MATLAB Command Window to the MS-DOS operating system environment in order to run temporary assignments. Entering the command ! *dos_command* in the Command Window allows you to run the specified DOS command in the MATLAB environment. For example:

```
! dir
```

```
The volume of drive D has no label
The volume serial number £ is 145 c-12F2
Directory of D:\MATLAB52\bin

.                      <DIR>     13/03/98   0:16 .
..                     <DIR>     13/03/98   0:16 ..
BCCOPTS   BAT           1.872    19/01/98   14:14 bccopts.bat
CLBS110   DLL         219.136    21/08/97   22:24 clbs110.dll
CMEX      BAT           2.274    13/03/98   0:28 cmex.bat
COMPTOOL  BAT          34.992    19/01/98   14:14 comptool.bat
DF500PTS  BAT           1.973    19/01/98   14:14 df50opts.bat
FENG      DLL          25.088    18/12/97   16:34 feng.dll
FMAT      DLL          16.896    18/12/97   16:34 fmat.dll
FMEX      BAT           2.274    13/03/98   0:28 fmex.bat
LICENSE   DAT             470    13/03/98   0:27 license.dat
W32SSI    DLL          66.560    02/05/97   8:34 w32ssi.dll
10 file(s)        11.348.865 bytes
directory(s) 159.383.552 bytes free
```

The command ! *dos_command* & is used to execute the specified DOS command in background mode. The command is executed by opening a DOS environment window on the MATLAB Command Window, as shown in Figure 1-20. To return to the MATLAB environment simply right-click anywhere in the Command Window (the DOS environment window will close automatically). You can return to the DOS window at any time to run any operating system command by clicking the icon labeled *MS-DOS symbol* at the bottom of the screen.

Figure 1-20.

The command >>*dos_command* is used to execute the DOS command in the MATLAB screen. Using the three previous commands, not only DOS commands, but also all kinds of executable files or batch tasks can be executed.

The command >>*dos dos_command* is also used to execute the specified DOS command in automatic mode in the MATLAB Command Window.

To exit MATLAB, simply type *quit* in the Command Window, and then press *Enter*.

CHAPTER 2

Variables, Numbers, Operators and Functions

Variables

MATLAB does not require a command to declare variables. A variable is created simply by directly allocating a value to it. For example:

```
>> v = 3

v =

3
```

The variable v will take the value 3 and using a new mapping will not change its value. Once the variable is declared, we can use it in calculations.

```
>> v ^ 3

ans =

27

>> v + 5

ans =

8
```

The value assigned to a variable remains fixed until it is explicitly changed or if the current MATLAB session is closed.

If we now write:

```
>> v = 3 + 7

v =

10
```

then the variable v has the value 10 from now on, as shown in the following calculation:

```
>> v ^ 4
```

ans =

10000

A variable name must begin with a letter followed by any number of letters, digits or underscores. However, bear in mind that MATLAB uses only the first 31 characters of the name of the variable. It is also very important to note that MATLAB is case sensitive. Therefore, a variable named with uppercase letters is different to the variable with the same name except in lowercase letters.

Vector Variables

A vector variable of n elements can be defined in MATLAB in the following ways:

```
V = [v1, v2, v3,..., vn]
```

```
V = [v1 v2 v3... vn]
```

When most MATLAB commands and functions are applied to a vector variable the result is understood to be that obtained by applying the command or function to each element of the vector:

```
>> vector1 = [1,4,9,2.25,1/4]
```

vector1 =

1.0000 4.0000 9.0000 2.2500 0.2500

```
>> sqrt (vector1)
```

ans =

1.0000 2.0000 3.0000 1.5000 0.5000

The following table presents some alternative ways of defining a vector variable without explicitly bracketing all its elements together, separated by commas or blank spaces.

variable = [a:b]	*Defines the vector whose first and last elements are a and b, respectively, and the intermediate elements differ by one unit.*
variable = [a:s:b]	*Defines the vector whose first and last elements are a and b, respectively, and the intermediate elements differ by an increase specified by s.*
variable = linespace [a, b, n]	*Defines the vector with n evenly spaced elements whose first and last elements are a and b respectively.*
variable = logspace [a, b, n]	*Defines the vector with n evenly logarithmically spaced elements whose first and last elements are 10a and 10b, respectively.*

Below are some examples:

```
>> vector2 = [5:5:25]
```

vector2 =

5 10 15 20 25

This yields the numbers between 5 and 25, inclusive, separated by 5 units.

```
>> vector3 = [10:30]
```

vector3 =

Columns 1 through 13

10   11   12   13   14   15   16   17   18   19   20   21   22

Columns 14 through 21

23 24 25 26 27 28 29 30

This yields the numbers between 10 and 30, inclusive, separated by a unit.

```
>> t:Microsoft.WindowsMobile.DirectX.Vector4 = linspace (10,30,6)
```

t:Microsoft.WindowsMobile.DirectX.Vector4 =

10 14 18 22 26 30

This yields 6 equally spaced numbers between 10 and 30, inclusive.

```
>> vector5 = logspace (10,30,6)
```

vector5 =

1. 0e + 030 *

0.0000 0:0000 0.0000 0.0000 0.0001 1.0000

This yields 6 evenly logarithmically spaced numbers between 10^{10} and 10^{30}, inclusive.

One can also consider row vectors and column vectors in MATLAB. A column vector is obtained by separating its elements by semicolons, or by transposing a row vector using a single quotation mark at the end of its definition.

```
>> a = [10;20;30;40]
```

a =

10
20
30
40

```
>> a = (10:14);b=a'
```

b =

```
10
11
12
13
14
```

```
>> c = (a')'
```

c =

```
10 11 12 13 14
```

You can also select an element of a vector or a subset of elements. The rules are summarized in the following table:

x (n)	*Returns the n-th element of the vector x.*
x(a:b)	*Returns the elements of the vector x between the a-th and the b-th elements, inclusive.*
x(a:p:b)	*Returns the elements of the vector x located between the a-th and the b-th elements, inclusive, but separated by p units (a > b).*
x(b:-p:a)	*Returns the elements of the vector x located between the b-th and a-th elements, both inclusive, but separated by p units and starting with the b-th element (b > a).*

Here are some examples:

```
>> x = (1:10)
```

x =

```
1    2    3    4    5    6    7    8    9    10
```

```
>> x (6)
```

ans =

```
6
```

This yields the sixth element of the vector *x*.

```
>> x(4:7)
```

ans =

```
4 5 6 7
```

This yields the elements of the vector x located between the fourth and seventh elements, inclusive.

>> x(2:3:9)

ans =

2 5 8

This yields the three elements of the vector x located between the second and ninth elements, inclusive, but separated in steps of three units.

>> x(9:-3:2)

ans =

9 6 3

This yields the three elements of the vector x located between the ninth and second elements, inclusive, but separated in steps of three units and starting at the ninth.

Matrix Variables

MATLAB defines arrays by inserting in brackets all its row vectors separated by a semicolon. Vectors can be entered by separating their components by spaces or by commas, as we already know. For example, a 3 × 3 matrix variable can be entered in the following two ways:

M = [a11 a12 a13;a21 a22 a23;a31 a32 a33]

M = [a11,a12,a13;a21,a22,a23;a31,a32,a33]

Similarly we can define an array of variable dimension *(M×N)*. Once a matrix variable has been defined, MATLAB enables many ways to insert, extract, renumber, and generally manipulate its elements. The following table shows different ways to define matrix variables.

A(m,n)	*Defines the (m, n)-th element of the matrix A (row m and column n).*
A(a:b,c:d)	*Defines the subarray of A formed between the a-th and the b-th rows and between the c-th and the d-th columns, inclusive.*
A(a:p:b,c:q:d)	*Defines the subarray of A formed by every p-th row between the a-th and the b-th rows, inclusive, and every q-th column between the c-th and the d-th column, inclusive.*
A([a b],[c d])	*Defines the subarray of A formed by the intersection of the a-th through b-th rows and c-th through d-th columns, inclusive.*
A([a b c...],[e f g...])	*Defines the subarray of A formed by the intersection of rows a, b, c,...and columns e, f, g,...*
A(:,c:d)	*Defines the subarray of A formed by all the rows in A and the c-th through to the d-th columns.*
A(:,[c d e...])	*Defines the subarray of A formed by all the rows in A and columns c, d, e,...*
A(a:b,:)	*Defines the subarray of A formed by all the columns in A and the a-th through to the b-th rows.*

(*continued*)

A([a b c...],:)	*Defines the subarray of A formed by all the columns in A and rows a, b, c,...*
A(a,:)	*Defines the a-th row of the matrix A.*
A(:,b)	*Defines the b-th column of the matrix A.*
A(:)	*Defines a column vector whose elements are the columns of A placed in order below each other.*
A(:,:)	*This is equivalent to the entire matrix A.*
[A, B, C,...]	*Defines the matrix formed by the matrices A, B, C,...*
S$_A$ = [ ]	*Clears the subarray of the matrix A, S$_A$, and returns the remainder.*
diag (v)	*Creates a diagonal matrix with the vector v in the diagonal.*
diag (A)	*Extracts the diagonal of the matrix as a column vector.*
eye (n)	*Creates the identity matrix of order n.*
eye (m, n)	*Creates an m×n matrix with ones on the main diagonal and zeros elsewhere.*
zeros (m, n)	*Creates the zero matrix of order m×n.*
ones (m, n)	*Creates the matrix of order m×n with all its elements equal to 1.*
rand (m, n)	*Creates a uniform random matrix of order m×n.*
randn (m, n)	*Creates a normal random matrix of order m×n.*
flipud (A)	*Returns the matrix whose rows are those of A but placed in reverse order (from top to bottom).*
fliplr (A)	*Returns the matrix whose columns are those of A but placed in reverse order (from left to right).*
rot90 (A)	*Rotates the matrix A counterclockwise by 90 degrees.*
reshape(A,m,n)	*Returns an m×n matrix formed by taking consecutive entries of A by columns.*
size (A)	*Returns the order (size) of the matrix A.*
find (cond$_A$)	*Returns all A items that meet a given condition.*
length (v)	*Returns the length of the vector v.*
tril (A)	*Returns the lower triangular part of the matrix A.*
triu (A)	*Returns the upper triangular part of the matrix A.*
A'	*Returns the transpose of the matrix A.*
Inv (A)	*Returns the inverse of the matrix A.*

Here are some examples:

We consider first the *2 × 3* matrix whose rows are the first six consecutive odd numbers:

```
>> A = [1 3 5; 7 9 11]
```

A =

1 3 5
7 9 11

Now we are going to change the *(2,3)-th* element, i.e. the last element of *A*, to zero:

```
>> A(2,3) = 0
```

A =

```
1 3 5
7 9 0
```

We now define the matrix *B* to be the transpose of *A*:

```
>> B = A'
```

B =

```
1 7
3 9
5 0
```

We now construct a matrix *C*, formed by attaching the identity matrix of order 3 to the right of the matrix *B*:

```
>> C = [B eye (3)]
```

C =

```
1    7    1    0    0
3    9    0    1    0
5    0    0    0    1
```

We are going to build a matrix *D* by extracting the odd columns of the matrix *C*, a matrix *E* formed by taking the intersection of the first two rows of *C* and its third and fifth columns, and a matrix *F* formed by taking the intersection of the first two rows and the last three columns of the matrix *C*:

```
>> D = C(:,1:2:5)
```

D =

```
1 1 0
3 0 0
5 0 1
```

```
>> E = C([1 2],[3 5])
```

E =

```
1 0
0 0
```

```
>> F = C([1 2],3:5)
```

F =

```
1 0 0
0 1 0
```

Now we build the diagonal matrix *G* such that the elements of the main diagonal are the same as those of the main diagonal of *D*:

```
>> G = diag(diag(D))
```

G =

```
1 0 0
0 0 0
0 0 1
```

We then build the matrix *H*, formed by taking the intersection of the first and third rows of *C* and its second, third and fifth columns:

```
>> H = C([1 3],[2 3 5])
```

H =

```
7 1 0
0 0 1
```

Now we build an array *I* formed by the identity matrix of order 5×4, appending the zero matrix of the same order to its right and to the right of that the unit matrix, again of the same order. Then we extract the first row of *I* and, finally, form the matrix *J* comprising the odd rows and even columns of *I* and calculate its order (size).

```
>> I = [eye(5,4) zeros(5,4) ones(5,4)]
```

ans =

```
1   0   0   0   0   0   0   0   1   1   1   1
0   1   0   0   0   0   0   0   1   1   1   1
0   0   1   0   0   0   0   0   1   1   1   1
0   0   0   1   0   0   0   0   1   1   1   1
0   0   0   0   0   0   0   0   1   1   1   1
```

```
>> I(1,:)
```

ans =

```
1   0   0   0   0   0   0   0   1   1   1   1
```

```
>> J=I(1:2:5,2:2:12)
```

J =

```
0    0    0    0    1    1
0    0    0    0    1    1
0    0    0    0    1    1
```

```
>> size(J)
```

ans =

3 6

We now construct a random matrix *K* of order *3 ×4*, reverse the order of the rows of *K*, reverse the order of the columns of *K* and then perform both operations simultaneously. Finally, we find the matrix *L* of order *4 × 3* whose columns are obtained by taking the elements of *K* sequentially by columns.

```
>> K=rand(3,4)
```

K =

```
0.5269    0.4160    0.7622    0.7361
0.0920    0.7012    0.2625    0.3282
0.6539    0.9103    0.0475    0.6326
```

```
>> K(3:-1:1,:)
```

ans =

```
0.6539    0.9103    0.0475    0.6326
0.0920    0.7012    0.2625    0.3282
0.5269    0.4160    0.7622    0.7361
```

```
>> K(:,4:-1:1)
```

ans =

```
0.7361    0.7622    0.4160    0.5269
0.3282    0.2625    0.7012    0.0920
0.6326    0.0475    0.9103    0.6539
```

```
>> K(3:-1:1,4:-1:1)
```

ans =

```
0.6326    0.0475    0.9103    0.6539
0.3282    0.2625    0.7012    0.0920
0.7361    0.7622    0.4160    0.5269
```

```
>> L=reshape(K,4,3)
```

L =

```
0.5269  0.7012  0.0475
0.0920  0.9103  0.7361
0.6539  0.7622  0.3282
0.4160  0.2625  0.6326
```

Character Variables

A character variable (chain) is simply a character string enclosed in single quotes that MATLAB treats as a vector form. The general syntax for character variables is as follows:

c = 'string'

Among the MATLAB commands that handle character variables we have the following:

abs ('character_string')	*Returns the array of ASCII characters equivalent to each character in the string.*
setstr (numeric_vector)	*Returns the string of ASCII characters that are equivalent to the elements of the vector.*
str2mat (t1,t2,t3,...)	*Returns the matrix whose rows are the strings t1, t2, t3,..., respectively*
str2num ('string')	*Converts the string to its exact numeric value used by MATLAB.*
num2str (number)	*Returns the exact number in its equivalent string with fixed precision.*
int2str (integer)	*Converts the integer to a string.*
sprintf ('format', a)	*Converts a numeric array into a string in the specified format.*
sscanf ('string', 'format')	*Converts a string to a numeric value in the specified format.*
dec2hex (integer)	*Converts a decimal integer into its equivalent string in hexadecimal.*
hex2dec ('string_hex')	*Converts a hexadecimal string into its integer equivalent.*
hex2num ('string_hex')	*Converts a hexadecimal string into the equivalent IEEE floating point number.*
lower ('string')	*Converts a string to lowercase.*
upper ('string')	*Converts a string to uppercase.*
strcmp (s1, s2)	*Compares the strings s1 and s2 and returns 1 if they are equal and 0 otherwise.*
strcmp (s1, s2, n)	*Compares the strings s1 and s2 and returns 1 if their first n characters are equal and 0 otherwise.*
strrep (c, 'exp1', 'exp2')	*Replaces exp1 by exp2 in the chain c.*
findstr (c, 'exp')	*Finds where exp is in the chain c.*
isstr (expression)	*Returns 1 if the expression is a string and 0 otherwise.*
ischar (expression)	*Returns 1 if the expression is a string and 0 otherwise.*
strjust (string)	*Right justifies the string.*

(*continued*)

blanks (n)	*Generates a string of n spaces.*
deblank (string)	*Removes blank spaces from the right of the string.*
eval (expression)	*Executes the expression, even if it is a string.*
disp ('string')	*Displays the string (or array) as has been written, and continues the MATLAB process.*
input ('string')	*Displays the string on the screen and waits for a key press to continue.*

Here are some examples:

>> **hex2dec ('3ffe56e')**

ans =

67102062

Here MATLAB has converted a hexadecimal string into a decimal number.

>> **dec2hex (1345679001)**

ans =

50356E99

The program has converted a decimal number into a hexadecimal string.

>> **sprintf('%f',[1+sqrt(5)/2,pi])**

ans =

2.118034 3.141593

The exact numerical components of a vector have been converted to strings (with default precision).

>> **sscanf('121.00012', '%f')**

ans =

121.0001

Here a numeric string has been passed to an exact numerical format (with default precision).

>> **num2str (pi)**

ans =

3.142

The constant π has been converted into a string.

```
>> str2num('15/14')
```

ans =

1.0714

The string has been converted into a numeric value with default precision.

```
>> setstr(32:126)
```

ans =

*!"#$% &' () * +, -. / 0123456789:; < = >? @ABCDEFGHIJKLMNOPQRSTUVWXYZ [\ ] ^*
_ 'abcdefghijklmnopqrstuvwxyz {|}~

This yields the ASCII characters associated with the whole numbers between 32 and 126, inclusive.

```
>> abs('{]}><#¡¿?ºª')
```

ans =

123 93 125 62 60 35 161 191 63 186 170

This yields the integers corresponding to the ASCII characters specified in the argument of *abs*.

```
>> lower ('ABCDefgHIJ')
```

ans =

abcdefghij

The text has been converted to lowercase.

```
>> upper('abcd eFGHi jKlMn')
```

ans =

ABCD EFGHI JKLMN

The text has been converted to uppercase.

```
>> str2mat ('The world',' The country',' Daily 16', ' ABC')
```

ans =

The world
The country
Daily 16
ABC

The chains comprising the arguments of *str2mat* have been converted to a text array.

```
>> disp('This text will appear on the screen')
```

ans =

This text will appear on the screen

Here the argument of the command *disp* has been displayed on the screen.

```
>> c = 'This is a good example';
>> strrep(c, 'good', 'bad')
```

ans =

This is a bad example

The string *good* has been replaced by *bad* in the chain *c*. The following instruction locates the initial position of each occurrence of *is* within the chain *c*.

```
>> findstr (c, 'is')
```

ans =

3 6

Numbers

In MATLAB the arguments of a function can take many different forms, including different types of numbers and numerical expressions, such as integers and rational, real and complex numbers.

Arithmetic operations in MATLAB are defined according to the standard mathematical conventions. MATLAB is an interactive program that allows you to perform a simple variety of mathematical operations. MATLAB assumes the usual operations of sum, difference, product, division and power, with the usual hierarchy between them:

x + y	*Sum*
x y	*Difference*
x * y or x y	*Product*
x/y	*Division*
x ^ y	*Power*

To add two numbers simply enter the first number, a plus sign (+) and the second number. Spaces may be included before and after the sign to ensure that the input is easier to read.

```
>> 2 + 3
```

ans =

5

We can perform power calculations directly.

```
>> 100 ^ 50
```

ans =

1. 0000e + 100

Unlike a calculator, when working with integers, MATLAB displays the full result even when there are more digits than would normally fit across the screen. For example, MATLAB returns the following value of *99 ^ 50* when using the vpa function (here to the default accuracy of 32 significant figures).

```
>> vpa '99 ^ 50'
```

ans =

. 60500606713753665044791996801256e100

To combine several operations in the same instruction one must take into account the usual priority criteria among them, which determine the order of evaluation of the expression. Consider, for example:

```
>> 2 * 3 ^ 2 + (5-2) * 3
```

ans =

27

Taking into account the priority of operators, the first expression to be evaluated is the power *3^2*. The usual evaluation order can be altered by grouping expressions together in parentheses.

In addition to these arithmetic operators, MATLAB is equipped with a set of basic functions and you can also define your own functions. MATLAB functions and operators can be applied to symbolic constants or numbers.

One of the basic applications of MATLAB is its use in realizing arithmetic operations as if it were a conventional calculator, but with one important difference: the precision of the calculation. Operations are performed to whatever degree of precision the user desires. This unlimited precision in calculation is a feature which sets MATLAB apart from other numerical calculation programs, where the accuracy is determined by a word length inherent to the software, and cannot be modified.

The accuracy of the output of MATLAB operations can be relaxed using special approximation techniques which are exact only up to a certain specified degree of precision. MATLAB represents results with accuracy, but even if internally you are always working with exact calculations to prevent propagation of rounding errors, different approximate representation formats can be enabled, which sometimes facilitate the interpretation of the results. The commands that allow numerical approximation are the following:

format long	*Delivers results to 16 significant decimal figures.*
format short	*Delivers results to 4 decimal places. This is MATLAB's default format.*
format long e	*Provides the results to 16 decimal figures more than the power of 10 required.*
format short e	*Provides the results to four decimal figures more than the power of 10 required.*
format long g	*Provides the results in optimal long format.*

(*continued*)

format short g	*Provides the results in optimum short format.*
bank format	*Delivers results to 2 decimal places.*
format rat	*Returns the results in the form of a rational number approximation.*
format +	*Returns the sign (+, -) and ignores the imaginary part of complex numbers.*
format hex	*Returns results in hexadecimal format.*
vpa 'operations' n	*Returns the result of the specified operations to n significant digits.*
numeric ('expr')	*Provides the value of the expression numerically approximated by the current active format.*
digits (n)	*Returns results to n significant digits.*

Using *format* gives a numerical approximation of 174/13 in the way specified after the format command:

```
>> 174/13
```

ans =

13.3846

```
>> format long; 174/13
```

ans =

13.38461538461539

```
>> format long e; 174/13
```

ans =

1.338461538461539e + 001

```
>> format short e; 174/13
```

ans =

1.3385e + 001

```
>> format long g; 174/13
```

ans =

13.3846153846154

```
>> format short g; 174/13
```

ans =

13.385

```
>> format bank; 174/13
```

ans =

13.38

```
>> format hex; 174/13
```

ans =

402ac4ec4ec4ec4f

Now we will see how the value of *sqrt (17)* can be calculated to any precision that we desire:

```
>> vpa ' 174/13 ' 10
```

ans =

13.38461538

```
>> vpa ' 174/13 ' 15
```

ans =

13.3846153846154

```
>> digits (20); vpa ' 174/13 '
```

ans =

13.384615384615384615

Integers

In MATLAB all common operations with whole numbers are exact, regardless of the size of the output. If we want the result of an operation to appear on screen to a certain number of significant figures, we use the symbolic computation command ***vpa*** (*variable precision arithmetic*), whose syntax we already know.

For example, the following calculates 6^400 to 450 significant figures:

```
>> '6 vpa ^ 400' 450
```

ans =

18217977168218728251394687124089371267338971528174760667459697549333959972090532700302826780076628386733147959945591636745242157445605964680105495406215017704234999886990788594743994796171248406730973807365248505631155692085087859428300809999273107625073394840473935055193456574397967882415119723262994774858 1376.

The result of the operation is precise, always displaying a point at the end of the result. In this case it turns out that the answer has fewer than 450 digits anyway, so the solution is exact. If you require a smaller number of significant figures, that number can be specified and the result will be rounded accordingly. For example, calculating the above power to only 50 significant figures we have:

```
>> '6 vpa ^ 400' 50
```

ans =

. *182179771682187282513946871240893712673389715281750e312*

Functions of Integers and Divisibility

There are several functions in MATLAB with integer arguments, the majority of which are related to divisibility. Among the most typical functions with integer arguments are the following:

rem (n, m)	*Returns the remainder of the division of n by m (also valid when n and m are real).*
sign (n)	*The sign of n (i.e. 1 if n > 0, - 1 if n < 0).*
max (n1, n2)	*The maximum of n1 and n2.*
min (n1, n2)	*The minimum of n1 and n2.*
gcd (n1, n2)	*The greatest common divisor of n1 and n2.*
lcm (n1, n2)	*The least common multiple of n1 and n2.*
factorial (n)	*n factorial (i.e. n(n-1) (n-2)...1)*
factor (n)	*Returns the prime factorization of n.*

Below are some examples.
The remainder of division of 17 by 3:

```
>> rem (17,3)
```

ans =

2

The remainder of division of 4.1 by 1.2:

```
>> rem (4.1,1.2)
```

ans =

0.5000

The remainder of division of -4.1 by 1.2:

```
>> rem (-4.1,1.2)
```

ans =

-0.5000

The greatest common divisor of 1000, 500 and 625:

```
>> gcd (1000, gcd (500,625))
```

ans =

125.00

The least common multiple of 1000, 500 and 625:

```
>> lcm (1000, lcm (500,625))
```

ans =

5000.00

Alternative Bases

MATLAB allows you to work with numbers to any base, as long as the extended symbolic math *Toolbox* is available. It also allows you to express all kinds of numbers in different bases. This is implemented via the following functions:

dec2base (decimal, n_base)	*Converts the specified decimal number to the new base n_base.*
base2dec(number,b)	*Converts the given number in base b to a decimal number.*
dec2bin (decimal)	*Converts the specified decimal number to base 2 (binary).*
dec2hex (decimal)	*Converts the specified decimal number to base 16 (hexadecimal).*
bin2dec (binary)	*Converts the specified binary number to decimal.*
hex2dec (hexadecimal)	*Converts the specified base 16 number to decimal.*

Below are some examples.
Represent in base 10 the base 2 number 100101.

```
>> base2dec ('100101',2)
```

ans =

37.00

Represent in base 10 the hexadecimal number FFFFAA00.

```
>> base2dec ('FFFFAA0', 16)
```

ans =

268434080.00

Represent the result of the base 16 operation FFFAA2+FF-1 in base 10.

```
>> base2dec ('FFFAA2',16) + base2dec('FF',16)-1
```

ans =

16776096.00

Real Numbers

As is well known, the set of real numbers is the disjoint union of the set of rational numbers and the set of irrational numbers. A rational number is a number of the form p/q, where p and q are integers. In other words, the rational numbers are those numbers that can be represented as a quotient of two integers. The way in which MATLAB treats rational numbers differs from the majority of calculators. If we ask a calculator to calculate the sum $1/2 + 1/3 + 1/4$, most will return something like *1.0833*, which is no more than an approximation of the result.

The rational numbers are ratios of integers, and MATLAB can work with them in exact mode, so the result of an arithmetic expression involving rational numbers is always given precisely as a ratio of two integers. To enable this, activate the rational format with the command *format rat*. If the reader so wishes, MATLAB can also return the results in decimal form by activating any other type of format instead (e.g. *format short* or *format long*). MATLAB evaluates the above mentioned sum in exact mode as follows:

```
>> format rat
>> 1/2 + 1/3 + 1/4
```

ans =

13/12

Unlike calculators, MATLAB ensures its operations with rational numbers are accurate by maintaining the rational numbers in the form of ratios of integers. In this way, calculations with fractions are not affected by rounding errors, which can become very serious, as evidenced by the theory of errors. Note that, once the rational format is enabled, when MATLAB adds two rational numbers the result is returned in symbolic form as a ratio of integers, and operations with rational numbers will continue to be exact until an alternative format is invoked.

A floating point number, or a number with a decimal point, is interpreted as exact if the rational format is enabled. Thus a floating point expression will be interpreted as an exact rational expression while any irrational numbers in a rational expression will be represented by an appropriate rational approximation.

```
>> format rat
>> 10/23 + 2.45/44
```

ans =

1183 / 2412

The other fundamental subset of the real numbers is the set of irrational numbers, which have always created difficulties in numerical calculation due to their special nature. The impossibility of representing an irrational number accurately in numeric mode (using the ten digits from the decimal numbering system) is the cause of most of the problems. MATLAB represents the results with an accuracy which can be set as required by the user. An irrational number, by definition, cannot be represented exactly as the ratio of two integers. If ordered to calculate the square root of 17, by default MATLAB returns the number 5.1962.

```
>> sqrt (27)
```

ans =

5.1962

MATLAB incorporates the following common irrational constants and notions:

pi	*The number π = 3.1415926...*
exp (1)	*The number e = 2.7182818...*
Inf	*Infinity (returned, for example, when it encounters 1/0).*
NaN	*Uncertainty (returned, for example, when it encounters 0/0).*
realmin	*Returns the smallest possible normalized floating-point number in IEEE double precision.*
realmax	*Returns the largest possible finite floating-point number in IEEE double precision.*

The following examples illustrate how MATLAB outputs these numbers and notions.

```
>> long format
>> pi
```

ans =

3.14159265358979

```
>> exp (1)
```

ans =

2.71828182845905

```
>> 1/0
```

Warning: Divide by zero.

ans =

Inf

```
>> 0/0
```

Warning: Divide by zero.

ans =

NaN

>> **realmin**

ans =

2. 225073858507201e-308

>> **realmax**

ans =

1. 797693134862316e + 308

Functions with Real Arguments

The disjoint union of the set of rational numbers and the set of irrational numbers is the set of real numbers. In turn, the set of rational numbers has the set of integers as a subset. All functions applicable to real numbers are also valid for integers and rational numbers. MATLAB provides a full range of predefined functions, most of which are discussed in the subsequent chapters of this book. Within the group of functions with real arguments offered by MATLAB, the following are the most important:

Trigonometric functions

Function	Inverse
sin (x)	**asin (x)**
cos (x)	**acos (x)**
tan(x)	**atan(x)** and **atan2(y,x)**
csc (x)	**acsc (x)**
sec (x)	**asec (x)**
cot (x)	**acot (x)**

Hyperbolic functions

Function	Inverse
sinh (x)	**asinh (x)**
cosh(x)	**acosh(x)**
tanh(x)	**atanh(x)**
csch(x)	**acsch(x)**
sech(x)	**asech(x)**
coth (x)	**acoth (x)**

Exponential and logarithmic functions

Function	Meaning
exp (x)	*Exponential function in base e (e ^ x).*
log (x)	*Base e logarithm of x.*
log10 (x)	*Base 10 logarithm of x.*
log2 (x)	*Base 2 logarithm of x.*
pow2 (x)	*2 raised to the power x.*
sqrt (x)	*The square root of x.*

Numeric variable-specific functions

Function	Meaning
abs (x)	*The absolute value of x.*
floor (x)	*The largest integer less than or equal to x.*
ceil (x)	*The smaller integer greater than or equal to x.*
round (x)	*The closest integer to x.*
fix (x)	*Removes the fractional part of x.*
rem (a, b)	*Returns the remainder of the division of a by b.*
sign (x)	*Returns the sign of x (1 if x > 0,0 if x=0,- 1 if x < 0).*

Here are some examples:

>> sin(pi/2)

ans =

1

>> asin (1)

ans =

1.57079632679490

>> log (exp (1) ^ 3)

ans =

3.00000000000000

The function *round* is demonstrated in the following two examples:

```
>> round (2.574)
```

ans =

3

```
>> round (2.4)
```

ans =

2

The function *ceil* is demonstrated in the following two examples:

```
>> ceil (4.2)
```

ans =

5

```
>> ceil (4.8)
```

ans =

5

The function *floor* is demonstrated in the following two examples:

```
>> floor (4.2)
```

ans =

4

```
>> floor (4.8)
```

ans =

4

The *fix* function simply removes the fractional part of a real number:

```
>> fix (5.789)
```

ans =

5

Complex Numbers

Operations on complex numbers are well implemented in MATLAB. MATLAB follows the convention that i or j represents the key value in complex analysis, the *imaginary number* $\sqrt{-1}$. All the usual arithmetic operators can be applied to complex numbers, and there are also some specific functions which have complex arguments. Both the real and the imaginary part of a complex number can be a real number or a symbolic constant, and operations with them are always performed in exact mode, unless otherwise instructed or necessary, in which case an approximation of the result is returned. As the imaginary unit is represented by the symbol i or j, the complex numbers are expressed in the form $a+bi$ or $a+bj$. Note that you don't need to use the product symbol (asterisk) before the imaginary unit:

```
>> (1-5i)*(1-i)/(-1+2i)
```

ans =

-1.6000 + 2.8000i

```
>> format rat
>> (1-5i) *(1-i) /(-1+2i)
```

ans =

-8/5 + 14/5i

Functions with Complex Arguments

Working with complex variables is very important in mathematical analysis and its many applications in engineering. MATLAB implements not only the usual arithmetic operations with complex numbers, but also various complex functions. The most important functions are listed below.

Trigonometric functions

Function	Inverse
sin (z)	asin (z)
cos (z)	acos (z)
tan (z)	atan(z) and atan2(imag(z),real(z))
csc (z)	acsc (z)
sec (z)	asec (z)
cot (z)	acot (z)

Hyperbolic functions

Function	Inverse
sinh (z)	asinh (z)
cosh(z)	acosh(z)
tanh(z)	atanh(z)
csch(z)	acsch(z)
sech(z)	asech(z)
coth (z)	acoth (z)

Exponential and logarithmic functions

Function	Meaning
exp (z)	*Exponential function in base e (e ^ z)*
log (z)	*Base e logarithm of z*
log10 (z)	*Base 10 logarithm of z.*
log2 (z)	*Base 2 logarithm of z.*
pow2 (z)	*2 to the power z.*
sqrt (z)	*The square root of z.*

Specific functions for the real and imaginary part

Function	Meaning
floor (z)	*Applies the floor function to real(z) and imag(z).*
ceil (z)	*Applies the ceil function to real(z) and imag(z).*
round (z)	*Applies the round function to real(z) and imag(z).*
fix (z)	*Applies the fix function to real(z) and imag(z).*

Specific functions for complex numbers

Function	Meaning
abs (z)	*The complex modulus of z.*
angle (z)	*The argument of z.*
conj (z)	*The complex conjugate of z.*
real (z)	*The real part of z.*
imag (z)	*The imaginary part of z.*

Below are some examples of operations with complex numbers.

```
>> round(1.5-3.4i)
```

ans =

2   -   3i

```
>> real(i^i)
```

ans =

0.2079

```
>> (2+2i)^2/(-3-3*sqrt(3)*i)^90
```

ans =

0502e-085 - 1 + 7. 4042e-070i

```
>> sin (1 + i)
```

ans =

1.2985 + 0. 6350i

Elementary Functions that Support Complex Vector Arguments

MATLAB easily handles vector and matrix calculus. Indeed, its name, *MAtrix LABoratory*, already gives an idea of its power in working with vectors and matrices. MATLAB allows you to work with functions of a complex variable, but in addition this variable can even be a vector or a matrix. Below is a table of functions with complex vector arguments.

max (V)	*The maximum component of V. (max is calculated for complex vectors as the complex number with the largest complex modulus (magnitude), computed with max(abs(V)). Then it computes the largest phase angle with max(angle(x)), if necessary.)*
min (V)	*The minimum component of V. (min is calculated for complex vectors as the complex number with the smallest complex modulus (magnitude), computed with min(abs(A)). Then it computes the smallest phase angle with min(angle(x)), if necessary.)*
mean (V)	*Average of the components of V.*
median (V)	*Median of the components of V.*
std (V)	*Standard deviation of the components of V.*
sort (V)	*Sorts the components of V in ascending order. For complex entries the order is by absolute value and argument.*
sum (V)	*Returns the sum of the components of V.*
prod (V)	*Returns the product of the components of V, so, for example, n! = prod(1:n).*
cumsum (V)	*Gives the cumulative sums of the components of V.*
cumprod (V)	*Gives the cumulative products of the components of V.*
diff (V)	*Gives the vector of first differences of V (V_t - V_{t-1}).*
gradient (V)	*Gives the gradient of V.*
del2 (V)	*Gives the Laplacian of V (5-point discrete).*
fft (V)	*Gives the discrete Fourier transform of V.*
fft2 (V)	*Gives the two-dimensional discrete Fourier transform of V.*
ifft (V)	*Gives the inverse discrete Fourier transform of V.*
ifft2 (V)	*Gives the inverse two-dimensional discrete Fourier transform of V.*

These functions also support a complex matrix as an argument, in which case the result is a vector of column vectors whose components are the results of applying the function to each column of the matrix.

Here are some examples:

```
>> V = 2:7, W = [5 + 3i 2-i 4i]
```

V =

2   3   4   5   6   7

W =

2.0000 - 1.0000i   0 + 4.0000i   5.0000 + 3.0000i

>> **diff(V),diff(W)**

ans =

1   1   1   1   1

ans =

-2.0000 + 5.0000i   5.0000 - 1.0000i

>> **cumprod(V),cumsum(V)**

ans =

2   6   24   120   720   5040

ans =

2   5   9   14   20   27

>> **cumsum(W), mean(W), std(W), sort(W), sum(W)**

ans =

2.0000 - 1.0000i   2.0000 + 3.0000i   7.0000 + 6.0000i

ans =

2.3333 + 2.0000i

ans =

3.6515

ans =

2.0000 - 1.0000i   0 + 4.0000i   5.0000 + 3.0000i

ans =

7.0000 + 6.0000i

>> **mean(V), std(V), sort(V), sum(V)**

ans =

4.5000

ans =

1.8708

ans =

2   3   4   5   6   7

ans =

27

```
>> fft(W), ifft(W), fft2(W)
```

ans =

7.0000 + 6.0000i   0.3660 - 0.1699i   -1.3660 - 8.8301i

ans =

2.3333 + 2.0000i -0.4553 - 2.9434i   0.1220 - 0.0566i

ans =

7.0000 + 6. 0000i 0.3660 - 0. 1699i -1.3660 - 8. 8301i

Elementary Functions that Support Complex Matrix Arguments

- **Trigonometric**

sin (z)	*Sine function*
sinh (z)	*Hyperbolic sine function*
asin (z)	*Arcsine function*
asinh (z)	*Hyperbolic arcsine function*
cos (z)	*Cosine function*
cosh (z)	*Hyperbolic cosine function*
acos (z)	*Arccosine function*
acosh (z)	*Hyperbolic arccosine function*
tan(z)	*Tangent function*
tanh (z)	*Hyperbolic tangent function*
atan (z)	*Arctangent function*
atan2 (z)	*Fourth quadrant arctangent function*
atanh (z)	*Hyperbolic arctangent function*

(*continued*)

sec (z)	*Secant function*
sech (z)	*Hyperbolic secant function*
asec (z)	*Arccosecant function*
asech (z)	*Hyperbolic arccosecant function*
csc (z)	*Cosecant function*
csch (z)	*Hyperbolic cosecant function*
acsc (z)	*Arccosecant function*
acsch (z)	*Hyperbolic arccosecant function*
cot (z)	*Cotangent function*
coth (z)	*Hyperbolic cotangent function*
acot (z)	*Arccotangent function*
acoth (z)	*Hyperbolic arccotangent function*
• **Exponential**	
exp (z)	*Base e exponential function*
log (z)	*Natural logarithm function (base e)*
log10 (z)	*Base 10 logarithm function*
sqrt (z)	*Square root function*
• **Complex**	
abs (z)	*Modulus or absolute value*
angle (z)	*Argument*
conj (z)	*Complex conjugate*
imag (z)	*Imaginary part*
real (z)	*Real part*
• **Numerical**	
fix (z)	*Removes the fractional part*
floor (z)	*Rounds to the nearest lower integer*
ceil (z)	*Rounds to the nearest greater integer*
round (z)	*Performs common rounding*
rem (z1, z2)	*Returns the remainder of the division of z1 by z2*
sign (z)	*The sign of z*

(continued)

- • *Matrix*

expm (Z)	*Matrix exponential function by default*
expm1 (Z)	*Matrix exponential function in M-file*
expm2 (Z)	*Matrix exponential function via Taylor series*
expm3 (Z)	*Matrix exponential function via eigenvalues*
logm (Z)	*Logarithmic matrix function*
sqrtm (Z)	*Matrix square root function*
funm(Z,'function')	*Applies the function to the array Z*

Here are some examples:

```
>> A = [7 8 9; 1 2 3; 4 5 6], B = [1+2i 3+i;4+i,i]
```

A =

```
7    8    9
1    2    3
4    5    6
```

B =

```
1.0000 + 2.0000i    3.0000 + 1.0000i
4.0000 + 1.0000i         0 + 1.0000i
```

```
>> sin(A), sin(B), exp(A), exp(B), log(B), sqrt(B)
```

ans =

```
 0.6570    0.9894    0.4121
 0.8415    0.9093    0.1411
-0.7568   -0.9589   -0.2794
```

ans =

```
 3.1658 + 1.9596i    0.2178 - 1.1634i
-1.1678 - 0.7682i         0 + 1.1752i
```

ans =

*1.0e+003 ***

```
1.0966    2.9810    8.1031
0.0027    0.0074    0.0201
0.0546    0.1484    0.4034
```

ans =

-1.1312 + 2.4717i   10.8523 +16.9014i
29.4995 +45.9428i   0.5403 + 0.8415i

ans =

0.8047 + 1.1071i   1.1513 + 0.3218i
1.4166 + 0.2450i   0 + 1.5708i

ans =

1.2720 + 0.7862i   1.7553 + 0.2848i
2.0153 + 0.2481i   0.7071 + 0.7071i

The exponential functions, square root and logarithm used above apply to the array elementwise and have nothing to do with the matrix exponential and logarithmic functions that are used below.

>> expm(B), logm(A), abs(B), imag(B)

ans =

-27.9191 +14.8698i -20.0011 +12.0638i
-24.7950 + 17.6831i -17.5059 + 14.0445i

ans =

* 11.9650   12.8038 -19.9093*
-21.7328 -22.1157 44.6052
* 11.8921   12.1200 -21.2040*

ans =

2.2361 3.1623
4.1231 1.0000

ans =

2   1
1   1

>> fix(sin(B)), ceil(log(A)), sign(B), rem(A,3*ones(3))

ans =

* 3.0000 + 1.0000i   0 - 1.0000i*
-1.0000   0 + 1.0000i

```
ans =

2    3    3
0    1    2
2    2    2

ans =

0.4472 + 0.8944i   0.9487 + 0.3162i
0.9701 + 0.2425i        0 + 1.0000i

ans =

1    2    0
1    2    0
1    2    0
```

Random Numbers

MATLAB can easily generate (pseudo) random numbers. The function *rand* generates uniformly distributed random numbers and the function *randn* generates normally distributed random numbers. The most interesting features of MATLAB's random number generator are presented in the following table.

rand	*Returns a uniformly distributed random decimal number from the interval [0,1].*
rand (n)	*Returns an array of size n×n whose elements are uniformly distributed random decimal numbers from the interval [0,1].*
rand (m, n)	*Returns an array of dimension m×n whose elements are uniformly distributed random decimal numbers from the interval [0,1].*
rand (size (a))	*Returns an array of the same size as the matrix A and whose elements are uniformly distributed random decimal numbers from the interval [0,1].*
rand ('seed')	*Returns the current value of the uniform random number generator seed.*
rand('seed',n)	*Assigns to n the current value of the uniform random number generator seed.*
randn	*Returns a normally distributed random decimal number (mean 0 and variance 1).*
randn (n)	*Returns an array of dimension n×n whose elements are normally distributed random decimal numbers (mean 0 and variance 1).*
randn (m, n)	*Returns an array of dimension m×n whose elements are normally distributed random decimal numbers (mean 0 and variance 1).*
randn (size (a))	*Returns an array of the same size as the matrix A and whose elements are normally distributed random decimal numbers (mean 0 and variance 1).*
randn ('seed')	*Returns the current value of the normal random number generator seed.*
randn('seed',n)	*Assigns to n the current value of the uniform random number generator seed.*

Here are some examples:

```
>> [rand, rand (1), randn, randn (1)]
```

ans =

0.9501   0.2311   -0.4326   -1.6656

```
>> [rand(2), randn(2)]
```

ans =

0.6068   0.8913   0.1253   -1.1465
0.4860   0.7621   0.2877   1.1909

```
>> [rand(2,3), randn(2,3)]
```

ans =

0.3529 0.0099 0.2028 -0.1364 1.0668 -0.0956
0.8132 0.1389 0.1987 0.1139 0.0593 -0.8323

Operators

MATLAB features arithmetic, logical, relational, conditional and structural operators.

Arithmetic Operators

There are two types of arithmetic operators in MATLAB: matrix arithmetic operators, which are governed by the rules of linear algebra, and arithmetic operators on vectors, which are performed elementwise. The operators involved are presented in the following table.

Operator	Role played
+	*Sum of scalars, vectors, or matrices*
-	*Subtraction of scalars, vectors, or matrices*
*	*Product of scalars or arrays*
.*	*Product of scalars or vectors*
\	$A \backslash B = inv (A) * B$, *where A and B are matrices*
.\	$A. \backslash B = [B(i,j) /A (i, j)]$, *where A and B are vectors* $[dim (A) = dim (B)]$
/	*Quotient, or* $B/A = B * inv (A)$, *where A and B are matrices*
./	$A / B = [A(i,j)/b (i, j)]$, *where A and B are vectors* $[dim (A) = dim (B)]$
^	*Power of a scalar or matrix* (M^p)
.^	*Power of vectors* $(A. \wedge B = [A(i,j)^{B(i,j)}]$, *for vectors A and B)*

Simple mathematical operations between scalars and vectors apply the scalar to all elements of the vector according to the defined operation, and simple operators between vectors are performed element by element. Below is the specification of these operators:

$a = \{a1, a2,..., an\}, b = \{b1, b2,..., bn\}, c = scalar$	
$a + c = [a1 + c, a2 + c,..., an+c]$	*Sum of a scalar and a vector*
$a * c = [a1 * c, a2 * c,..., an * c]$	*Product of a scalar and a vector*
$a + b = [a1+b1 \quad a2+b2 ... an+bn]$	*Sum of two vectors*
$a. * b = [a1*b1 \quad a2*b2 ... an*bn]$	*Product of two vectors*
$a. / b = [a1/b1 \quad a2/b2 ... an/bn]$	*Ratio to the right of two vectors*
$a. \backslash b = [a1\backslash b1 \quad a2\backslash b2 ... an\backslash bn]$	*Ratio to the left of two vectors*
$a. \wedge c = [a1 \wedge c, a2 \wedge c,..., an \wedge c]$	*Vector to the power of a scalar*
$c. \wedge a = [c \wedge a1, c \wedge a2,..., c \wedge an]$	*Scalar to the power of a vector*
$a.\wedge b = [a1\wedge b1 \quad a2\wedge b2 ... an\wedge bn]$	*Vector to the power of a vector*

It must be borne in mind that the vectors must be of the same length and that in the product, quotient and power the first operand must be followed by a point.

The following example involves all of the above operators.

```
>> X = [5,4,3]; Y = [1,2,7]; a = X + Y, b = X-Y, c = x * Y, d = 2. * X,...
e = 2/X, f = 2. \Y, g = x / Y, h =. \X, i = x ^ 2, j = 2. ^ X, k = X. ^ Y

a =

6       6       10

b =

4       2       -4

c =

5       8       21

d =

10      8       6

e =

0.4000    0.5000    0.6667

f =

0.5000    1.0000    3.5000
```

g =

5.0000   2.0000   0.4286

h =

5.0000   2.0000   0.4286

i =

25   16   9

j =

32 16 8

k =

5 16 2187

The above operations are all valid since in all cases the variable operands are of the same dimension, so the operations are successfully carried out element by element. For the sum and the difference there is no distinction between vectors and matrices, as the operations are identical in both cases.

The most important operators for matrix variables are specified below:

A + B, A - B, A * B	*Addition, subtraction and product of matrices.*
A\B	*If A is square, A\B = inv (A) * B. If A is not square, A\B is the solution, in the sense of least-squares, of the system AX = B.*
B/A	*Coincides with (A ' \ B')'.*
Aⁿ	*Coincides with A * A * A *... *A n times (n integer).*
pᴬ	*Performs the power operation only if p is a scalar.*

Here are some examples:

```
>> X = [5,4,3]; Y = [1,2,7]; l = X'* Y, m = X * Y ', n = 2 * X, o = X / Y, p = Y\X
```

l =

5 10 35
4 8 28
3 6 21

m =

34

n =

10 8 6

o =

0.6296

p =

0	*0*	*0*
0	*0*	*0*
0.7143	*0.5714*	*0.4286*

All of the above matrix operations are well defined since the dimensions of the operands are compatible in every case. We must not forget that a vector is a particular case of matrix, but to operate with it in matrix form (not element by element), it is necessary to respect the rules of dimensionality for matrix operations. For example, the vector operations $X.'*Y$ and $X.*Y'$ make no sense, since they involve vectors of different dimensions. Similarly, the matrix operations $X*Y$, $2/X$, $2\backslash Y$, $X\wedge 2$, $2\wedge X$ and $X\wedge Y$ make no sense, again because of a conflict of dimensions in the arrays.

Here are some more examples of matrix operators.

>> M = [1,2,3;1,0,2;7,8,9]

M =

1 2 3
1 0 2
7 8 9

>> B = inv (M), C = M ^ 2, D = M ^(1/2), E = 2 ^ M

B =

-0.8889	*0.3333*	*0.2222*
0.2778	*-0.6667*	*0.0556*
0.4444	*0.3333*	*-0.1111*

C =

24	*26*	*34*
15	*18*	*21*
78	*86*	*118*

D =

0.5219 + 0.8432i	*0.5793 - 0.0664i*	*0.7756 - 0.2344i*
0.3270 + 0.0207i	*0.3630 + 1.0650i*	*0.4859 - 0.2012i*
1.7848 - 0.5828i	*1.9811 - 0.7508i*	*2.6524 + 0.3080i*

E =

*1. 0e + 003 ***

0.8626 0.9568 1.2811
0.5401 0.5999 0.8027
2.9482 3.2725 4.3816

Relational Operators

MATLAB also provides relational operators. Relational operators perform element by element comparisons between two matrices and return an array of the same size whose elements are zero if the corresponding relationship is true, or one if the corresponding relation is false. The relational operators can also compare scalars with vectors or matrices, in which case the scalar is compared to all the elements of the array. Below is a table of these operators.

<	*Less than (for complex numbers this applies only to the real parts)*
< =	*Less than or equal (only applies to real parts of complex numbers)*
>	*Greater than (only applies to real parts of complex numbers)*
> =	*Greater than or equal (only applies to real parts of complex numbers)*
x == y	*Equality (also applies to complex numbers)*
x ~ = y	*Inequality (also applies to complex numbers)*

Logical Operators

MATLAB provides symbols to denote logical operators. The logical operators shown in the following table offer a way to combine or negate relational expressions.

~ A	*Logical negation (NOT) or the complement of A.*
A & B	*Logical conjunction (AND) or the intersection of A and B.*
A | B	*Logical disjunction (OR) or the union of A and B.*
XOR (A, B)	*Exclusive OR (XOR) or the symmetric difference of A and B (takes the value 1 if A or B, but not both, are 1).*

Here are some examples:

>> A = 2:7;P =(A>3) &(A<6)

P =

0   0   1   1   0   0

Returns 1 when the corresponding element of *A* is greater than 3 and less than 6, and returns 0 otherwise.

```
>> X = 3 * ones (3.3); X > = [7 8 9; 4 5 6 ; 1 2 3]

ans =

0 0 0
0 0 0
1 1 1
```

The elements of the solution array corresponding to those elements of *X* which are greater than or equal to the equivalent entry of the matrix *[7 8 9; 4 5 6; 1 2 3]* are assigned the value 1. The remaining elements are assigned the value 0.

Logical Functions

MATLAB implements logical functions whose output can take the value true (1) or false (0). The following table shows the most important logical functions.

exist(A)	*Checks if the variable or function exists (returns 0 if A does not exist and a number between 1 and 5, depending on the type, if it does exist).*
any (V)	*Returns 0 if all elements of the vector V are null and returns 1 if some element of V is non-zero.*
any (A)	*Returns 0 for each column of the matrix A with all null elements and returns 1 for each column of the matrix A which has non-null elements.*
all (V)	*Returns 1 if all the elements of the vector V are non-null and returns 0 if some element of V is null.*
all (A)	*Returns 1 for each column of the matrix A with all non-null elements and returns 0 for each column of the matrix A with at least one null element.*
find (V)	*Returns the places (or indices) occupied by the non-null elements of the vector V.*
isnan (V)	*Returns 1 for the elements of V that are indeterminate and returns 0 for those that are not.*
isinf (V)	*Returns 1 for the elements of V that are infinite and returns 0 for those that are not.*
isfinite (V)	*Returns 1 for the elements of V that are finite and returns 0 for those that are not.*
isempty (A)	*Returns 1 if A is an empty array and returns 0 otherwise (an empty array is an array such that one of its dimensions is 0).*
issparse (A)	*Returns 1 if A is a sparse matrix and returns 0 otherwise.*
isreal (V)	*Returns 1 if all the elements of V are real and 0 otherwise.*
isprime (V)	*Returns 1 for all elements of V that are prime and returns 0 for all elements of V that are not prime.*
islogical (V)	*Returns 1 if V is a logical vector and 0 otherwise.*
isnumeric (V)	*Returns 1 if V is a numeric vector and 0 otherwise.*
ishold	*Returns 1 if the properties of the current graph are retained for the next graph and only new elements will be added and 0 otherwise.*
isieee	*Returns 1 if the computer is capable of IEEE standard operations.*

(continued)

isstr (S)	*Returns 1 if S is a string and 0 otherwise.*
ischart (S)	*Returns 1 if S is a string and 0 otherwise.*
isglobal (A)	*Returns 1 if A is a global variable and 0 otherwise.*
isletter (S)	*Returns 1 if S is a letter of the alphabet and 0 otherwise.*
isequal (A, B)	*Returns 1 if the matrices or vectors A and B are equal, and 0 otherwise.*
ismember(V, W)	*Returns 1 for every element of V which is in W and 0 for every element V that is not in W.*

Below are some examples using the above defined logical functions.

```
>> V = [1,2,3,4,5,6,7,8,9], isprime(V), isnumeric(V), all(V), any(V)

V =

1    2    3    4    5    6    7    8    9

ans =

0    1    1    0    1    0    1    0    0

ans =

1

ans =

1

ans =

1

>> B = [Inf, -Inf, pi, NaN], isinf(B), isfinite(B), isnan(B), isreal(B)

B =

Inf - Inf 3.1416 NaN

ans =

1 1 0 0

ans =

0 0 1 0
```

ans =

0 0 0 1

ans =

1


```
>> ismember ([1,2,3], [8,12,1,3]), A = [2,0,1];B = [4,0,2]; isequal (2A * B)
```

ans =

1 0 1

ans =

1

EXERCISE 2-1

Find the number of ways of choosing 12 elements from 30 without repetition, the remainder of the division of 2^{134} by 3, the prime decomposition of 18900, the factorial of 200 and the smallest number n which when divided by 16,24,30 and 32 leaves remainder 5.

```
>> factorial (30) / (factorial (12) * factorial(30-12))
```

ans =

8.6493e + 007

The command *vpa* is used to present the exact result.

```
>> vpa 'factorial (30) / (factorial (12) * factorial(30-12))' 15
```

ans =

86493225.

```
>> rem(2^134,3)
```

ans =

0

```
>> factor (18900)
```

ans =

2   2   3   3   3   5   5   7

```
>> factorial (100)
```

ans =

9. 3326e + 157

The command *vpa* is used to present the exact result.

```
>> vpa ' factorial (100)' 160
```

ans =

9332621544394415268169923885626670049071596826438162146859296389521759999322991560894146397615651828625369792082722375825118521091686400000000000000000000000.

N-5 is the least common multiple of 16, 24, 30 and 32.

```
>> lcm (lcm (16.24), lcm (30,32))
```

ans =

480

Then N = 480 + 5 = 485.

EXERCISE 2-2

In base 5 find the result of the operation defined by $a25aaff6_{16} + 6789aba_{12} + 35671_8 + 1100221_3 - 1250$. In base 13 find the result of the operation $(666551_7)* (aa199800a_{11}) + (fffaaa125_{16}) / (33331_4 + 6)$.

The result of the first operation in base 10 is calculated as follows:

```
>> base2dec('a25aaf6',16) + base2dec('6789aba',12) +...
base2dec('35671',8) + base2dec('1100221',3)-1250
```

ans =

190096544

We then convert this to base 5:

```
>> dec2base (190096544,5)
```

ans =

342131042134

Thus, the final result of the first operation in base 5 is 342131042134.

The result of the second operation in base 10 is calculated as follows:

```
>> base2dec('666551',7) * base2dec('aa199800a',11) +...
79 * base2dec('fffaaa125',16) / (base2dec ('33331', 4) + 6)
```

ans =

2. 7537e + 014

We now transform the result obtained into base 13.

```
>> dec2base (275373340490852,13)
```

ans =

BA867963C1496

EXERCISE 2-3

In base 13, find the result of the following operation: $(666551_7)* (aa199800a_{11}) + (fffaaa125_{16}) / (33331_4 + 6)$.

First, we perform the operation in base 10:

A more direct way of doing all of the above is:

```
>> base2dec('666551',7) * base2dec('aa199800a',11) +...
79 * base2dec('fffaaa125',16) / (base2dec ('33331', 4) + 6)
```

ans =

2. 753733404908515e + 014

We now transform the result obtained into base 13.

```
>> dec2base (275373340490852,13)
```

ans =

BA867963C1496

EXERCISE 2-4

Given the complex numbers X = 2 + 2i and Y=-3-3√3 i, calculate Y^3X^2/Y^{90}, $Y^{1/2}$, $Y^{3/2}$ and ln (X).

```
>> X=2+2*i; Y=-3-3*sqrt(3)*i;
>> Y^3
```

ans =

216

```
>> X ^ 2 / Y ^ 90
```

ans =

050180953422426e-085 - 1 + 7. 404188256695968e-070i

```
>> sqrt (Y)
```

ans =

1.22474487139159 - 2.12132034355964i

```
>> sqrt(Y^3)
```

ans =

14.69693845669907

```
>> log (X)
```

ans =

1.03972077083992 + 0.785398163397451i

EXERCISE 2-5

Calculate the value of the following operations with complex numbers:

$$\frac{i^8-i^{-8}}{3-4i}+1, \quad i^{\sin(1+i)}, \quad (2+\ln(i))^{\frac{1}{i}}, \quad (1+i)^i, \quad i^{\ln(1+i)}, \quad (1+\sqrt{3}i)^{1-i}$$

```
>> (i^8-i^(-8))/(3-4*i) + 1
```

ans =

1

```
>> i^(sin(1+i))
```

ans =

-0.16665202215166 + 0.329041394503307i

```
>> (2+log(i))^(1/i)
```

ans =

1.15809185259777 - 1.563880539890023i

```
>> (1+i)^i
```

ans =

0.42882900629437 + 0.154871752464425i

```
>> i^(log(1+i))
```

ans =

0.24911518828716 + 0.15081974884717i

```
>> (1+sqrt(3)*i)^(1-i)
```

ans =

5.34581479196611 + 1. 97594883452873i

EXERCISE 2-6

Calculate the real part, imaginary part, modulus and argument of each of the following expressions:

$$i^{3i}, \quad (1+\sqrt{3i})^{1-i}, \quad i^{i^i}, \quad i^i.$$

```
>> Z1 = i ^ 3 * i; Z2 = (1 + sqrt (3) * i) ^(1-i); Z3 =(i^i) ^ i;Z4 = i ^ i;
```

```
>> format short
```

```
>> real ([Z1 Z2 Z3 Z4])
```

ans =

1.0000 5.3458 0.0000 0.2079

>> imag ([Z1 Z2 Z3 Z4])

ans =

0 1.9759 - 1.0000 0

>> abs ([Z1 Z2 Z3 Z4])

ans =

1.0000 5.6993 1.0000 0.2079

>> angle ([Z1 Z2 Z3 Z4])

ans =

0 0.3541 - 1.5708 0

EXERCISE 2-7

Generate a square matrix of order 4 whose elements are uniformly distributed random numbers from [0,1].
Generate another square matrix of order 4 whose elements are normally distributed random numbers from [0,1].
Find the present generating seeds, change their value to ½ and rebuild the two arrays of random numbers.

>> rand (4)

ans =

0.9501 0.8913 0.8214 0.9218
0.2311 0.7621 0.4447 0.7382
0.6068 0.4565 0.6154 0.1763
0.4860 0.0185 0.7919 0.4057

>> randn (4)

ans =

-0.4326 -1.1465 0.3273 -0.5883
-1.6656 1.1909 0.1746 2.1832
0.1253 1.1892 -0.1867 -0.1364
0.2877 -0.0376 0.7258 0.1139

>> rand ('seed')

ans =

931316785

>> randn ('seed')

ans =

931316785

>> randn ('seed', 1/2)
>> rand ('seed', 1/2)
>> rand (4)

ans =

0.2190 0.9347 0.0346 0.0077
0.0470 0.3835 0.0535 0.3834
0.6789 0.5194 0.5297 0.0668
0.6793 0.8310 0.6711 0.4175

>> randn (4)

ans =

1.1650 -0.6965 0.2641 1.2460
0.6268 1.6961 0.8717 -0.6390
0.0751 0.0591 -1.4462 0.5774
0.3516 1.7971 -0.7012 -0.3600

EXERCISE 2-8

Given the vector variables a = [π, 2π, 3π, 4π, 5π] and b = [e, 2e, 3e, 4e, 5e], calculate c = sin (a) + b, d = cos (a), e = ln (b), f = c * d, g = c/d, h = d ^ 2, i = d ^ 2-e ^ 2 and j = 3d ^ 3-2e ^ 2.

*>> a = [pi, 2 * pi, 3 * pi, 4 * pi, 5 * pi],*
*b = [exp (1), 2 * exp (1), 3 * exp (1), 4 * exp (1),5*exp(1)],*
*c=sin(a)+b,d=cos(a),e=log(b),f=c.*d,g=c./d,]*
*h=d.^2, i=d.^2-e.^2, j=3*d.^3-2*e.^2*

a =

3.1416   6.2832   9.4248   12.5664   15.7080

b =

2.7183 5.4366 8.1548 10.8731 13.5914

c =

2.7183 5.4366 8.1548 10.8731 13.5914

d =

-1   1   -1   1   -1

e =

1.0000 1.6931 2.0986 2.3863 2.6094

f =

-2.7183 5.4366 - 8.1548 10.8731 - 13.5914

g =

-2.7183 5.4366 - 8.1548 10.8731 - 13.5914

h =

1   1   1   1   1

i =

0 - 1.8667 - 3.4042 - 4.6944 - 5.8092

j =

-5.0000 - 2.7335 - 11.8083 - 8.3888 - 16.6183

EXERCISE 2-9

Given a uniform random square matrix M of order 3, obtain its inverse, its transpose and its diagonal.
Transform it into a lower triangular matrix (replacing the upper triangular entries by 0) and rotate it 90 degrees
counterclockwise. Find the sum of the elements in the first row and the sum of the diagonal elements. Extract
the subarray whose diagonal elements are at $_{11}$ and $_{22}$ and also remove the subarray whose diagonal elements
are at $_{11}$ and $_{33}$.

```
>> M = rand(3)
```

M =

```
0.6868    0.8462    0.6539
0.5890    0.5269    0.4160
0.9304    0.0920    0.7012
```

```
>> A = inv(M)
```

A =

```
-4.1588     6.6947    -0.0934
 0.3255     1.5930    -1.2487
 5.4758    -9.0924     1.7138
```

```
>> B = M'
```

B =

```
0.6868     0.5890     0.9304
0.8462     0.5269     0.0920
0.6539     0.4160     0.7012
```

```
>> V = diag(M)
```

V =

```
0.6868
0.5269
0.7012
```

```
>> TI = tril(M)
```

TI =

```
0.6868     0          0
0.5890     0.5269     0
0.9304     0.0920     0.7012
```

```
>> TS = triu(M)
```

TS =

```
0.6868     0.8462     0.6539
0          0.5269     0.4160
0          0          0.7012
```

```
>> TR = rot90(M)
```

TR =

```
0.6539     0.4160     0.7012
0.8462     0.5269     0.0920
0.6868     0.5890     0.9304
```

```
>> s = M(1,1)+M(1,2)+M(1,3)
```

s =

```
2.1869
```

```
>> sd = M(1,1)+M(2,2)+M(3,3)
```

sd =

1.9149

```
>> SM = M(1:2,1:2)
```

SM =

0.6868 0.8462
0.5890 0.5269

```
>> SM1 = M([1 3], [1 3])
```

SM1 =

0.6868 0.6539
0.9304 0.7012

EXERCISE 2-10

Given the following complex square matrix M of order 3, find its square, its square root and its base 2 and − 2 exponential:

$$M = \begin{bmatrix} i & 2i & 3i \\ 4i & 5i & 6i \\ 7i & 8i & 9i \end{bmatrix}.$$

```
>> M = [i 2*i 3*i; 4*i 5*i 6*i; 7*i 8*i 9*i]
```

M =

0 + 1.0000i   0 + 2.0000i   0 + 3.0000i
0 + 4.0000i   0 + 5.0000i   0 + 6.0000i
0 + 7.0000i   0 + 8.0000i   0 + 9.0000i

```
>> C = M^2
```

C =

-30   -36   -42
-66   -81   -96
-102   -126   -150

```
>> D = M^(1/2)
```

D =

```
0.8570 - 0.2210i   0.5370 + 0.2445i   0.2169 + 0.7101i
0.7797 + 0.6607i   0.9011 + 0.8688i   1.0224 + 1.0769i
0.7024 + 1.5424i   1.2651 + 1.4930i   1.8279 + 1.4437i
```

```
>> 2^M
```

ans =

```
 0.7020 - 0.6146i  -0.1693 - 0.2723i  -0.0407 + 0.0699i
-0.2320 - 0.3055i   0.7366 - 0.3220i  -0.2947 - 0.3386i
-0.1661 + 0.0036i  -0.3574 - 0.3717i   0.4513 - 0.7471i
```

```
>> (-2)^M
```

ans =

```
 17.3946 -16.8443i    4.3404 -  4.5696i   -7.7139 + 7.7050i
  1.5685 -  1.8595i    1.1826 -  0.5045i   -1.2033 + 0.8506i
-13.2575 +13.1252i   -3.9751 +  3.5607i    6.3073 - 6.0038i
```

EXERCISE 2-11

Given the complex matrix M in the previous exercise, find its elementwise logarithm and its elementwise base e exponential. Also calculate the results of the matrix operations e^M and ln (M).

```
>> M = [i 2*i 3*i; 4*i 5*i 6*i; 7*i 8*i 9*i]
```

```
>> log(M)
```

ans =

```
0 + 1.5708i        0.6931 + 1.5708i   1.0986 + 1.5708i
1.3863 + 1.5708i   1.6094 + 1.5708i   1.7918 + 1.5708i
1.9459 + 1.5708i   2.0794 + 1.5708i   2.1972 + 1.5708i
```

```
>> exp(M)
```

ans =

```
 0.5403 + 0.8415i  -0.4161 + 0.9093i  -0.9900 + 0.1411i
-0.6536 - 0.7568i   0.2837 - 0.9589i   0.9602 - 0.2794i
 0.7539 + 0.6570i  -0.1455 + 0.9894i  -0.9111 + 0.4121i
```

```
>> logm(M)
```

ans =

```
-5.4033 - 0.8472i   11.9931 - 0.3109i  -5.3770 + 0.8846i
 12.3029 + 0.0537i -22.3087 + 0.8953i  12.6127 + 0.4183i
-4.7574 + 1.6138i   12.9225 + 0.7828i  -4.1641 + 0.6112i
```

```
>> expm(M)
```

ans =

```
 0.3802 - 0.6928i  -0.3738 - 0.2306i  -0.1278 + 0.2316i
-0.5312 - 0.1724i   0.3901 - 0.1434i  -0.6886 - 0.1143i
-0.4426 + 0.3479i  -0.8460 - 0.0561i  -0.2493 - 0.4602i
```

EXERCISE 2-12

Given the complex vector V = [1 + i, i, 1 -i], find the mean, median, standard deviation, variance, sum, product, maximum and minimum of its elements, as well as its gradient, its discrete Fourier transform and its inverse discrete Fourier transform.

```
>> [mean(V),median(V),std(V),var(V),sum(V),prod(V),max(V),min(V)]'
```

ans =

```
0.6667 - 0.3333i
1.0000 + 1.0000i
1.2910
1.6667
2.0000 - 1.0000i
0 - 2.0000i
1.0000 + 1.0000i
0 - 1.0000i
```

```
>> gradient(V)
```

ans =

```
1.0000 - 2.0000i   0.5000   0 + 2.0000i
```

```
>> fft(V)
```

ans =

```
2.0000 + 1.0000i  -2.7321 + 1.0000i   0.7321 + 1.0000i
```

```
>> ifft(V)
```

ans =

0.6667 + 0. 3333i 0.2440 + 0. 3333i - 0.9107 + 0. 3333i

EXERCISE 2-13

Given the arrays

$$A = \begin{bmatrix} 1 & 1 & 0 \\ 0 & 1 & 1 \\ 0 & 0 & 1 \end{bmatrix} \quad B = \begin{bmatrix} i & 1-i & 2+i \\ 0 & -1 & 3-i \\ 0 & 0 & -i \end{bmatrix} \quad C = \begin{bmatrix} 1 & 1 & 1 \\ 0 & sqrt(2)i & -sqrt(2)i \\ 1 & -1 & -1 \end{bmatrix}$$

calculate AB − BA, $A^2 + B^2 + C^2$, ABC, sqrt (A)+sqrt(B)+sqrt(C), $e^A(e^B + e^C)$, their transposes and their inverses. Also verify that the product of any of the matrices A, B, C with its inverse yields the identity matrix.

```
>> A = [1 1 0;0 1 1;0 0 1]; B=[i 1-i 2+i;0 -1 3-i;0 0 -i]; C=[1 1 1; 0 sqrt(2)*i
-sqrt(2)*i;1 -1 -1];
```

```
>> M1 = A*B-B*A
```

M1 =

0	-1.0000 - 1.0000i	2.0000
0	0	1.0000 - 1.0000i
0	0	0

```
>> M2 = A^2+B^2+C^2
```

M2 =

2.0000	2.0000 + 3.4142i	3.0000 - 5.4142i
0 - 1.4142i	-0.0000 + 1.4142i	0.0000 - 0.5858i
0	2.0000 - 1.4142i	2.0000 + 1.4142i

```
>> M3 = A*B*C
```

M3 =

5.0000 + 1.0000i	-3.5858 + 1.0000i	-6.4142 + 1.0000i
3.0000 - 2.0000i	-3.0000 + 0.5858i	-3.0000 + 3.4142i
0 - 1.0000i	0 + 1.0000i	0 + 1.0000i

```
>> M4 = sqrtm(A)+sqrtm(B)-sqrtm(C)
```

M4 =

```
 0.6356 + 0.8361i  -0.3250 - 0.8204i   3.0734 + 1.2896i
 0.1582 - 0.1521i   0.0896 + 0.5702i   3.3029 - 1.8025i
-0.3740 - 0.2654i   0.7472 + 0.3370i   1.2255 + 0.1048i
```

```
>> M5 = expm(A)*(expm(B)+expm(C))
```

M5 =

```
14.1906 - 0.0822i   5.4400 + 4.2724i  17.9169 - 9.5842i
 4.5854 - 1.4972i   0.6830 + 2.1575i   8.5597 - 7.6573i
 3.5528 + 0.3560i   0.1008 - 0.7488i   3.2433 - 1.8406i
```

```
>> inv(A)
```

ans =

```
1 -1  1
0 -1 -1
0  0  1
```

```
>> inv(B)
```

ans =

```
0 - 1.0000i  -1.0000 - 1.0000i  -4.0000 + 3.0000i
0             -1.0000            1.0000 + 3.0000i
0              0                 0 + 1.0000i
```

```
>> inv(C)
```

ans =

```
0.5000              0            0.5000
0.2500       0 - 0.3536i  -0.2500
0.2500       0 + 0.3536i  -0.2500
```

```
>> [A*inv(A) B*inv(B) C*inv(C)]
```

ans =

```
1    0    0    1    0    0    1    0    0
0    1    0    0    1    0    0    1    0
0    0    1    0    0    1    0    0    1
```

```
>> A'

ans =

1 0 0
1 1 0
0 1 1

>> B'

ans =

0 - 1.0000i        0              0
1.0000 + 1.0000i  -1.0000        0
2.0000 - 1.0000i   3.0000 + 1.0000i 0 + 1.0000i

>> C'

ans =

1.0000    0              1.0000
1.0000    0 - 1.4142i   -1.0000
1.0000    0 + 1.4142i   -1.0000
```

■ ▓ ▓

CHAPTER 3

Curves in Explicit, Parametric and Polar Coordinates. Surfaces

Introduction

MATLAB is a scientific software that implements high-performance graphics. It allows to you create two and three-dimensional graphs of exploratory data, graph curves in explicit, implicit and polar coordinates, plot surfaces in explicit, implicit, or parametric coordinates, draw mesh and contour plots, represent various geometric objects and create other specialized graphics.

You can freely adjust the graphics parameters, choosing such features as framing and positioning, line characteristics, markers, axes limits, mesh types, annotations, labels and legends. You can export graphics in many different formats. All of these features will be described in this chapter.

Exploratory Graphics

MATLAB incorporates commands that allow you to create basic exploratory graphics, such as histograms, bar charts, graphs, arrow diagrams, etc. The following table summarizes these commands. For all of them, it is necessary to first define the field of variation of the variable.

---

bar(Y)   *Creates a bar chart relative to the vector of frequencies Y. If Y is a matrix it creates multiple bar charts for each row of Y.*

```
>> x = [1 2 5 8 4 3 4 1 2 3 2];
>> bar (x)
```

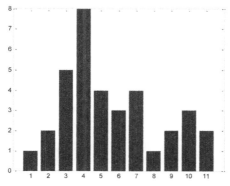

(*continued*)

bar(x,Y)   *Creates a bar chart relative to the vector of frequencies Y where x is a vector that defines the location of the bars on the x-axis.*

```
>> x = -2.9:0.2:2.9;
>> bar (x, exp(-x.*x))
```

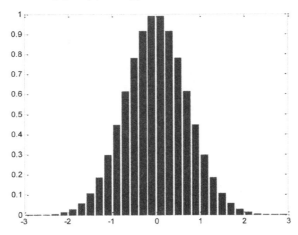

bar(...,width)   *Creates a bar chart where the bars are given the specified width. By default, the width is 0.8. A width of 1 causes the bars to touch.*

(*continued*)

bar(..., 'style')	*Creates a bar chart with the given style of bars. The possible styles are 'group' (the default vertical bar style) and 'stack' (stacked horizontal bars). If the matrix is m× n, the bars are grouped in m groups of n bars.*

```
>> A = [1 6 12 5 7; 3 2 6 5 3];
>> bar (A, 'stack')
>> bar (A, 'group')
```

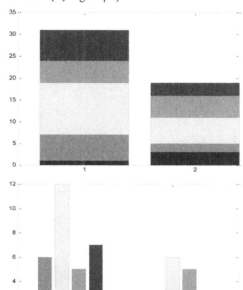

bar(..., color)	*Creates a bar chart where the bars are all of the specified color (r = red, g = green, b = blue, c = cyan, m = magenta, y = yellow, k = black and w = white).*
barh(...)	*Creates a horizontal bar chart.*

```
>> barh (A, 'group')
```

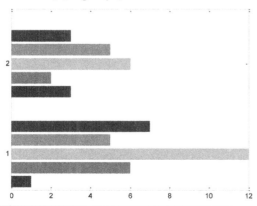

(continued)

hist(Y) *Creates a histogram relative to the vector of frequencies Y using 10 equal basis equally spaced rectangles. If Y is a matrix, a histogram is created for each of its columns.*

```
>> Y = randn(100);
>> hist(Y)
```

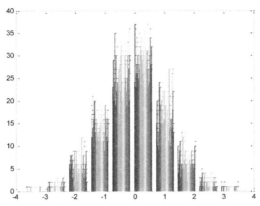

hist(Y,x) *Creates a histogram relative to the vector of frequencies Y where the number of bins is given by the number of elements in the vector x and the data is sorted according to vector x (if the entries of x are evenly spaced then these are used as the centers of the bins, otherwise the midpoints of successive values are used as the bin edges).*

hist(Y,k) *Creates histogram relative to the vector of frequencies Y using as many bins as indicated by the scalar k.*

```
>> hist(Y, 8)
```

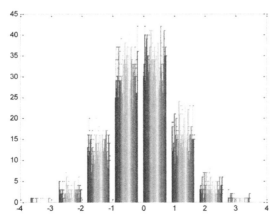

[n,x] = hist(…) *Returns the vectors n and x with the frequencies assigned to each bin of the histogram and the locations of the centers of each bin.*

(continued)

pie(X)   *Creates a pie chart relative to the vector of frequencies X*

```
>> X = [3 5 12 4 7 10];
>> pie(X)
```

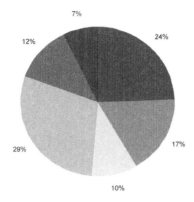

pie(X,Y)   *Creates a pie chart relative to the vector of frequencies X by moving out the sectors for which Yi ≠ 0.*

```
>> pie(X,[0 0 1 0 1 1])
```

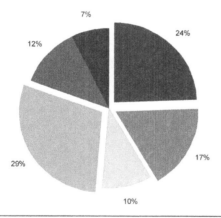

(continued)

errorbar(x,y,e)   *Plots the function y against x showing the error ranges specified by the vector e. To indicate the confidence intervals a vertical line of length 2ei is drawn passing through each point (x_i, y_i) with center (x_i, y_i).*

```
>> x = - 4:.2:4;
y = (1/sqrt(2*pi))*exp(-(x.^2)/2);
e = rand (size (x)) / 10;
errorbar(x,y,e)
```

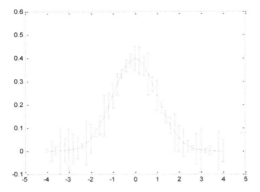

stem(Y)   *Plots the data sequence Y as stems extending from the x-axis baseline to the points indicated by a small circle.*

```
>> y = randn (50.1); stem (y)
```

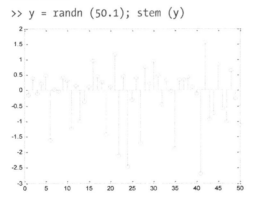

stem(X,Y)   *Plots the data sequence Y as a stem diagram with x-axis values determined by X.*

stairs(Y)   *Draws a stairstep graph of the data sequence Y.*

(*continued*)

stairs(X,Y)   *Plots a stairstep graph of the data Y where the x-values are determined by the vector X.*

```
>> x=-3:0.1:3; stairs(x,exp(-x.^2))
```

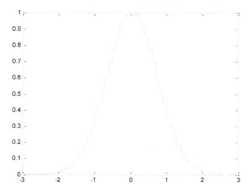

rose (Y)   *Creates an angle histogram showing the distribution of the data Y in 20 angle bins. The angles are given in radians. The radii reflect the number of elements falling into the corresponding bin.*

```
>> y = randn (1000,1) * pi; rose (y)
```

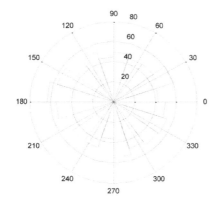

rose(Y,n)   *Plots an angle histogram of the data Y with n equally spaced bins. The default value of n is 20.*

rose(Y,X)   *Plots an angle histogram of the data Y where X specifies the number and location (central angle) of the bins.*

(continued)

compass(Z)   *Plots a compass diagram of the data Z. For each entry of the vector of complex numbers Z an arrow is drawn with base at the origin and head at the point determined by the entry.*

>> z=eig(randn(20,20)); compass(z)

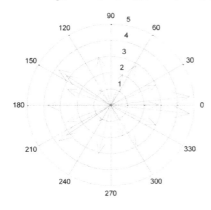

compass(X,Y)   *Equivalent to compass(X+i*Y).*

compass(Z, S) or   *Plots a compass diagram with arrow styles specified by S.*
compass(X, Y, S)

feather(Z) or   *Produces a plot similar to a compass plot, except the arrows now emanate from equally-spaced*
feather(X,Y) or   *points along the x-axis instead of from the origin.*
feather(Z,S) or
feather(X,Y,S)   >> z=eig(randn(20,20)); feather(z)

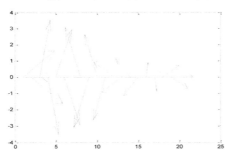

Curves in Explicit, Implicit, Parametric and Polar Coordinates

The most important MATLAB commands for plotting curves in two dimensions in explicit, polar and implied coordinates are presented in the following table.

plot(X,Y)	*Plots the set of points (X, Y), where X and Y are row vectors. For graphing a function y = f(x) it is necessary to specify a set of points (X, f(X)), where X is the range of variation of the variable x. X and Y can be arrays of the same size, in which case a graph is made by plotting the corresponding points (Xi,Yi) on the same axis. For complex values of X and Y the imaginary parts are ignored. For x = x(t) and y = y(t) with the given parameter t, the specified planar parametric curve graphic variation.* `>> x=0:0.1:6*pi; y=x.*sin(x); plot(x,y)` 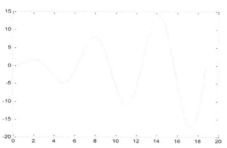
plot(Y)	*Creates a line plot of the vector Y against its indices. This is useful for plotting time series. If Y is a matrix plot(Y) creates a graph for each column of Y, presenting them all on the same axes. If the components of the vector are complex, plot(Y) is equivalent to plot(real(Y),imag(Y)).* `>> Y=[1,3,9,27,81,243,729]; plot(Y)` 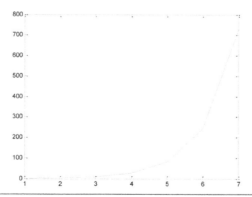

(continued)

plot(X, Y, S)	*Creates a plot of Y against X as described by plot(X,Y) with the settings defined in S. Usually S consists of two characters between single quotes, the first sets the color of the line graph and the second specfies the markeror line type. The possible values of colors and characters are, respectively, as follows: y (yellow), m (magenta), c (cyan), r (red), g (green), b (blue), w (white), k (black), . (point), o (circle), x (cross), s (square), d (diamond), ^ (upward pointing triangle), v (downward pointing triangle), > (right pointing triangle), < (left pointing triangle), p (pentagram), h (hexagram), + (plus sign), * (asterisk), - (solid line), -- (dashed line),: (dotted line), -. (dash-dot line).*

>> plot([1,2,3,4,5,6,7,8,9],[1, 1/2, 1/3,1/4,1/5,1/6, 1/7,1/8,1/9],'r *')

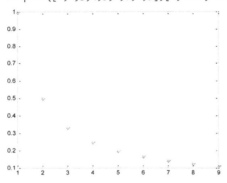

plot(X1,Y1,S1,X2,Y2,S2,...)	*Combines the plots for the triples (Xi, Yi, Si). This is a useful way of representing various functions on the same graph.*
fplot('f', [xmin, xmax])	*Graphs the explicit function y = f (x) in the specified range of variation for x.*

>> fplot('x*sin(1/x)', [0,pi/16])

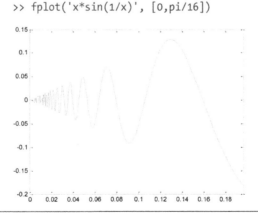

(continued)

fplot('f',[xmin, xmax, ymin, ymax], S)

Graphs the explicit function $y = f(x)$ in the specified intervals of variation for x and y, with options for color and characters given by S.

```
>> fplot('x^2/(x + 1)', [-12,12,-8, 8])
```

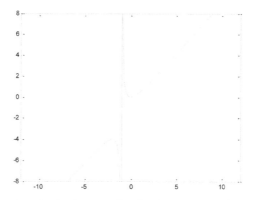

fplot('f',[xmin,xmax],...,t)

Graphs the function f with relative error tolerance t.

fplot('f',[xmin, xmax],...,n)

Graphs the function f with a minimum of $n + 1$ points where the maximum step size is (xmax-xmin)/nt.

fplot('[f1,f2,...,fn]',[xmin, xmax, ymin, ymax], S)

Graphs the functions f1, f2,..., fn on the same axes in the specified ranges of variation of x and y and with the color and markers given by S.

```
>> fplot('[sin(x), sin(2*x), sin(3*x)]', [0,2*pi])
```

```
>> fplot ('[sin (x), sin(2*x), sin(3*x)]', [0, 2 * pi],'k *')
```

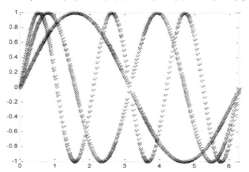

(*continued*)

ezplot('f' , [xmin, xmax])   *Graphs the explicit function y = f (x) or implicit function f(x,y) = k in the given range of variation of x. The range of variation of the variable can be omitted.*

```
>> ezplot('y*x^2 + x*y^2 = 10',[-10,10])
```

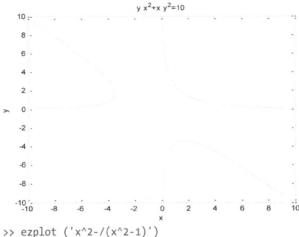

```
>> ezplot ('x^2-/(x^2-1)')
```

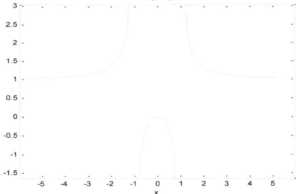

(continued)

ezplot('f', [xmin, xmax, ymin, ymax])

Graphs the explicit function $y = f(x)$ or the implicit function $f(x,y) = k$ for the given intervals of variation of x and y (which can be omitted).

```
>> ezplot('x^2 + y^3 = 1/2',[-10,10,-8,8])
```

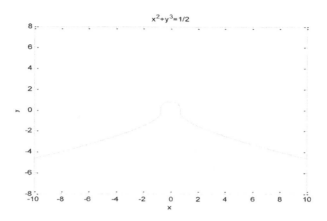

```
>> ezplot('x^2 - y^4 = 1')
```

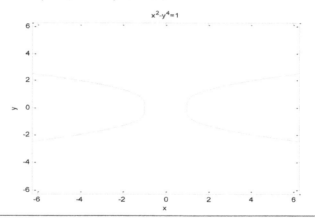

(*continued*)

ezplot(x,y)   *Graphs the planar parametric curve x = x(t) and y = y(t) for 0 ≤ t < 2 π*

```
>> ezplot ('4 * cos (t) - cos(4*t)', ' 4 * sin (t) - sin(4*t)')
```

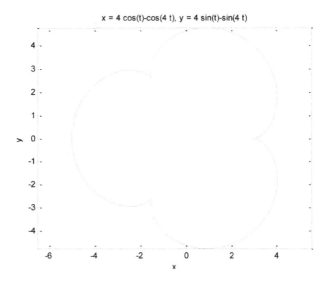

ezplot('f', [xmin xmax])   *Graphs the planar parametric curve x = x(t) and y = y(t) for xmin < t < xmax.*

```
>> ezplot('t*sin(t)', 't*cos(t)',[-4*pi,4*pi]
```

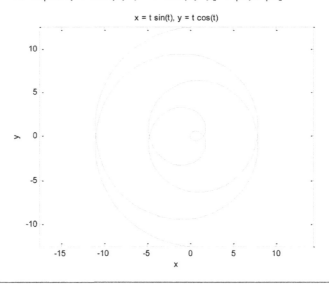

(continued)

ezplot('f')   *Graphs the curve f where the coordinates range over the default domain [-2 π,2 π].*
```
>> ezplot('y^4 - x^4 - 24*y^2 + 25*x^2 = 0')
```

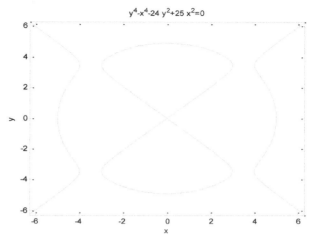

loglog(X,Y)   *Produces a plot similar to plot(X,Y), but with a logarithmic scale on the two axes.*
```
>> x=0:0.1:pi; y=x.*sin(x); loglog(x,y)
```

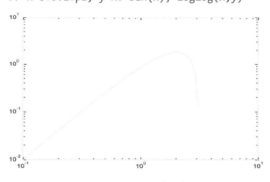

semilogx(X,Y)   *Produces a plot similar to plot(X,Y), but with a logarithmic scale on the x-axis and a normal scale on the y-axis.*
```
>> x=0:0.1:pi; y=x.*sin(x); semilogx(x,y)
```

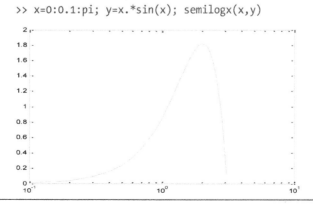

(continued)

| **semilogy(X,Y)** | *Produces a plot similar to plot(X,Y), but with a logarithmic scale on the y-axis and and a normal scale on the x-axis.* |

```
>> x=0:0.1:pi; y=x.*sin(x); semilogy(x,y)
```

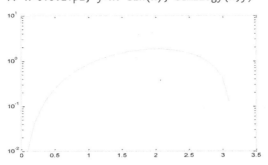

| **polar(α, r)** | *Draws the curve* $r = r(\alpha)$ *given in polar coordinates.* |

```
>> t=0:0.1:2*pi;r=sin(t).*cos(t); polar(t,r)
```

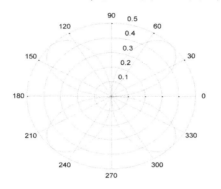

| **polar(α, r, S)** | *Draws the curve* $r = r(\alpha)$ *given in polar coordinates with the style of lines specified by S.* |

```
>> t=0:0.05:2*pi;r=sin(t).*cos(t); polar(t,r,'*r')
```

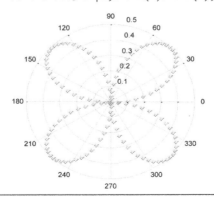

(continued)

ezpolar(r)

ezpolar(r, [a, b])

Draws the curve $r = r(\alpha)$ in polar coordinates where the field of variation of α is given by [a,b], or if it is not stated, is the default range [0, 2π].

```
>> ezpolar ('1 + cos (t)')
```

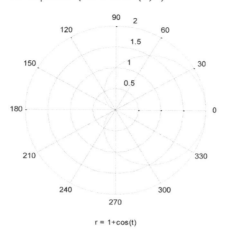

r = 1+cos(t)

fill(X, Y, C)

Draws the filled polygon whose vertices are given by the components (X_i, Y_i) of the specified vectors X and Y. The vector C, which is of the same size as X and Y, specifies the colors assigned to the corresponding points. The Ci values may be: 'r', 'g', 'b', 'c', 'm', 'y', 'w', 'k', whose meanings we already know. If C is a single character, all vertices of the polygon will be assigned the specified color. If X and Y are matrices of the same size then several polygons will be created, each corresponding to the columns of the matrices. In this case, C can be a row vector specifying the color of each polygon, or it can be a matrix specifying the color of the vertices of the polygons.

```
>> t = (1/16:1 / 8:1)'* 2 * pi; x = sin (t); y = cos (t); fill (x, y, 'r')
```

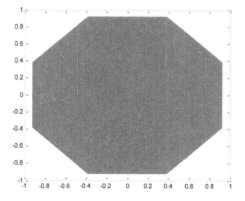

fill(X1,Y1,C1,...)

Draws the filled polygon with vertex coordinates and colors given by (X_i, Y_i, C_i).

Three-dimensional (3D) Curves

MATLAB includes commands that allow you to plot space curves in three dimensions. The following table presents the most important commands.

plot3(X, Y, Z)	*Draws a 3D line plot by joining the sequence of points determined by (X, Y, Z) by lines, where X, Y and Z are row vectors. X, Y and Z can also be parametric coordinates or matrices of the same size, in which case a graph is made for each triplet of rows, on the same axes. For complex values of X, Y and Z, the imaginary parts are ignored.*

```
>> X = [0 1 1 2; 1 1 2 2; 0 0 1 1];
Y = [1 1 1 1; 1 0 1 0; 0 0 0 0];
Z = [1 1 1 1; 1 0 1 0; 0 0 0 0];
>> plot3 (X, Y, Z)
```

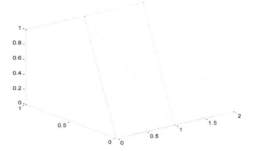

```
>> t = 0:pi/100:20 * pi; plot3 (2 * sin(2*t), 2 * cos(2*t), 4 * t)
```

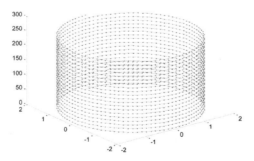

plot3(X, Y, Z, S)	*Produces the line plot plot(X,Y,Z) with the settings defined in S. S usually consists of two characters between single quotes, the first of which sets the color of the line graph and the second determines the line or marker properties. The possible settings have already been described above for the plot command.*
plot3(X1,Y1,Z1,S1, X2,Y2,Z2,S2,X3, Y3, Z3, S3,...)	*Combines 3D line plots for the quadruples (X_i, Y_i, Z_i, S_i) on the same axes. This is a useful way of representing various functions on the same graph.*

(continued)

fill3(X,Y,Z,C) *Draws the filled polygon whose vertices are given by the triples of components (X_i, Y_i, Z_i) of the column vectors X, Y and Z. C is a vector of the same size as X, Y and Z, which specifies the colour Ci at each vertex (X_i, Y_i, Z_i)). The Ci values can be 'r', 'g', 'b', 'c', 'm', 'y', 'w', 'k', whose meanings we already know. If C is a single character, all vertices will be given this color. If X, Y and Z are matrices of the same size, several polygons corresponding to each triplet column vector (X.j, Y.j, Z.j) will be drawn. In this case, C can be a row vector of elements Cj determining the unique color of each polygon corresponding to (X.j, Y.j, Z.j). C can also be a matrix of the same dimension as X, Y and Z, in which case its elements determine the colors of each vertex $(X_{ijk}, Y_{ijk}, Z_{ijk})$ of the set of polygons.*

```
>> X = [0 1 1 2; 1 1 2 2; 0 0 1 1];
Y = [1 1 1 1; 1 0 1 0; 0 0 0 0];
Z = [1 1 1 1; 1 0 1 0; 0 0 0 0];
C = [0.5000 1.0000 1.0000 0.5000;
1.0000 0.5000 0.5000 0.1667;
0.3330 0.3330 0.5000 0.5000];
fill3(X,Y,Z,C)
```

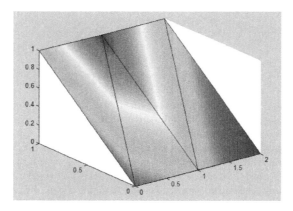

fill3(X1,Y1,Z1,C1, *Draws the filled polygon whose vertices and colors are given by (X_i, Y_i, Z_i, C_i).*
X2, Y2, Z2, C2,...)

(*continued*)

ezplot3(x(t), y(t), z(t))	*Draws the space curve defined by the given three parametric components.*
ezplot3(x(t),y(t),z(t), [tmin,tmax])	*Draws the space curve defined by the given three parametric components for the specified range of variation of the parameter.*

>> ezplot3 ('sin (t)', 'cos (t)', ', [0, 6 * pi])

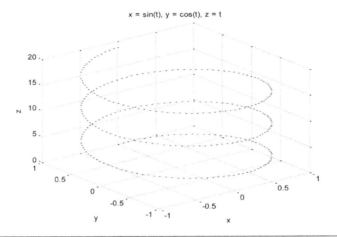

Explicit and Parametric Surfaces. Contour Plots

MATLAB includes commands that allow you to represent surfaces defined by equations of the form $z = f(x,y)$. The first step is to use the command *meshgrid*, which defines the array of points (X, Y) at which the function will be evaluated. Then the command *surf* is used to create the surface.

The command *mesh* is also used to produce a mesh plot that is defined by a function $z = f(x,y)$, so that the points on the surface are represented on a network determined by the z values given by $f(x,y)$ for corresponding points of the plane (x, y). The appearance of a mesh plot is like a fishing net, with surface points forming the nodes of the network.

It is also possible to represent the level curves of a surface by using the command *contour*. These curves are characterized as being the set of points (x,y) in the plane for which the value $f(x,y)$ is some fixed constant.

The following table lists the MATLAB commands which can be used to produce mesh and contour representations of surfaces both in explicit and parametric form.

[X, Y] = meshgrid(x,y)	*Creates a rectangular grid by transforming the monotonically increasing grid vectors x and y into two matrices X and Y specifying the entire grid. Such a grid can be used by the commands surf and mesh to produce surface graphics.*
surf(X,Y,Z,C)	*Represents the explicit surface $z = f(x,y)$ or the parametric surface $x = x(t,u)$, $y = y(t,u)$, $z = z(t,u)$, using the colors specified in C. The C argument can be omitted.*

```
>> [X, Y] = meshgrid(-2:.2:2,-2:.2:2);
Z = X. * exp(-X.^2-Y.^2); surf (X, Y, Z)
```

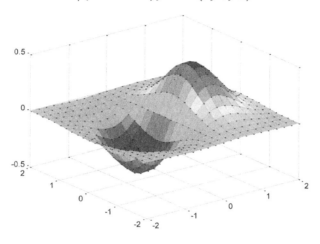

surfc(X,Y,Z,C)   *Represents the explicit surface $z = f(x,y)$ or the parametric surface $x = x(t,u)$, $y = y(t,u)$, $z = z(t,u)$, together with a contour plot of the surface. The contour lines are projected onto the xy-plane.*

```
>> [X, Y] = meshgrid(-2:.2:2,-2:.2:2);
Z = X. * exp(-X.^2-Y.^2); surfc (X, Y, Z)
```

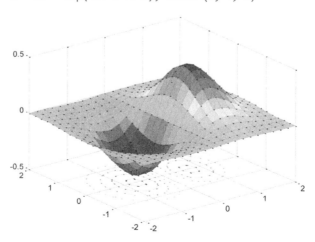

(continued)

| **surfl(X, Y, Z)** | *Represents the explicit surface z = f(x,y) or the parametric surface x = x(t,u), y = y(t,u), z = z(t,u), with colormap-based lighting.* |

```
>> r =(0:0.1:2*pi)';
t =(-pi:0.1:2*pi);
X = cos (r) * sin (t);
Y = sin (r) * sin (t);
Z = ones (size (r) 1)'* t;
surfl (X, Y, Z)
```

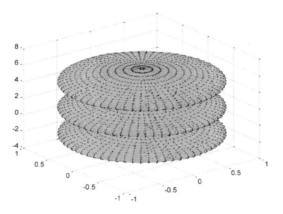

| **mesh(X,Y,Z,C)** | *Represents the explicit surface z = f(x,y) or the parametric surface x = x(t,u), y = y(t,u), z = z(t,u), drawing the grid lines that compose the mesh with the colors specified by C (optional).* |

```
>> [X, Y] = meshgrid(-2:.2:2,-2:.2:2);
Z = X. * exp(-X.^2-Y.^2); mesh (X, Y, Z)
```

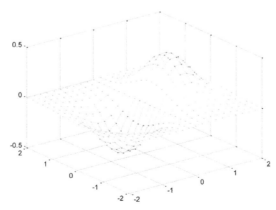

| **meshz(X,Y,Z,C)** | *Represents the explicit surface z = f(x,y) or the parametric surface x = x(t,u), y = y(t,u), z = z(t,u) adding a 'curtain' around the mesh.* |

(*continued*)

meshc(X,Y,Z,C)

Represents the explicit surface z = f(x,y) or the parametric surface x = x(t,u), y = y(t,u), z = z(t,u) together with a contour plot of the surface. The contour lines are projected on the xy-plane.

```
>> [X, Y] = m.2:.2:2,-2:.2:2);
Z = X. * exp(-X.^2-Y.^2); meshc (X, Y, Z)
```

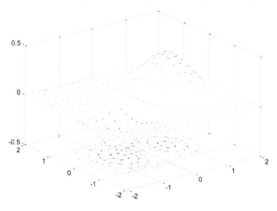

contour(Z)

Draws a contour plot of the matrix Z, where Z is interpreted as heights of the surface over the xy-plane. The number of contour lines is selected automatically.

```
>> [X, Y] = meshgrid(-2:.2:2,-2:.2:2);
Z = X. * exp(-X.^2-Y.^2);
>> contour (Z)
```

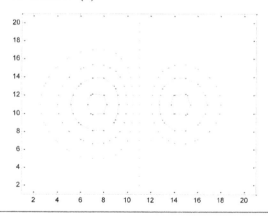

(*continued*)

contour(Z,n)

Draws a contour plot of the matrix Z using n contour lines.

```
>> [X, Y] = meshgrid(-2:.2:2,-2:.2:2);
Z = X. * exp(-X.^2-Y.^2);
>> contour (Z)
```

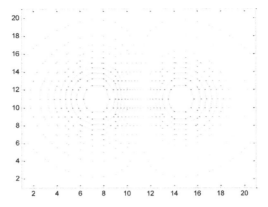

contour(x, y, Z, n)

Draws a contour plot of the matrix Z with n contour lines and using the x-axis and y-axis values specified by the vectors x and y.

```
>> r =(0:0.1:2*pi); t =(-pi:0.1:2*pi);
X = cos (r) * cos (t);Y = sin (r) * sin (t);Z = ones (size (r) 1)'* t;
>> contour (X, Y, Z)
```

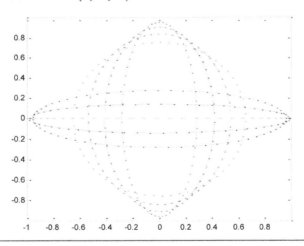

(continued)

102

contour3(Z),   *Draws three-dimensional contour plots.*

contour3(Z, n) y   >> r =(0:0.1:2*pi); t =(-pi:0.1:2*pi);

contour3(x, y, Z, n)   X = cos (r) * cos (t);Y = sin (r) * sin (t);Z = ones (size (r) 1)'* t;

>> contour3 (X, Y, Z)

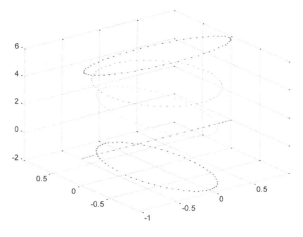

contourf(...)   *Draws a contour plot and fills in the areas between the isolines.*

>> r = (0:0.1:2*pi); t = (-pi:0.1:2*pi);

X = cos (r) * cos (t);Y = sin (r) * sin (t);Z = ones (size (r) 1)'* t;

>> contourf (X, Y, Z)

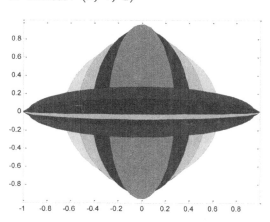

(continued)

pcolor(X, Y, Z)	*Draws a 'pseudocolor' contour plot determined by the matrix (X, Y, Z) using a color representation based on densities. This is often called a density plot.*

```
>> [X, Y] = meshgrid(-2:.2:2,-2:.2:2);
Z = X. * exp(-X.^2-Y.^2); meshc (X, Y, Z)
>> pcolor (X, Y, Z)
```

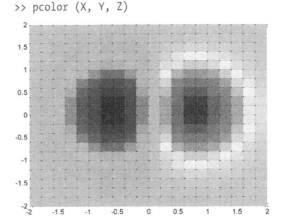

trimesh(Tri, X, Y, Z, C)	*Creates a triangular mesh plot. Each row of the matrix Tri defines a simple triangular face and C defines colors as in surf. The C argument is optional.*
trisurf(Tri,X,Y,Z,C)	*Creates a triangular surface plot. Each row of the matrix Tri defines a simple triangular face and C defines colors as in surf. The C argument is optional.*

Three-dimensional Geometric Forms

The representation of cylinders, spheres, bars, sections, stems, waterfall charts and other three-dimensional geometric objects is possible with MATLAB. The following table summarizes the commands that can be used for this purpose.

bar3 (Y)	*Creates a 3D bar graph relative to the vector of frequencies Y. If Y is a matrix, multiple bar graphs are produced on the same axes, one for each row of Y.*

```
>> bar3 (rand (4.4))
```

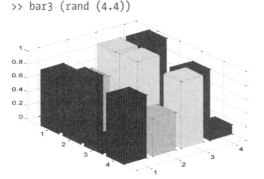

(*continued*)

bar3(x,Y)	*Creates a 3D bar graph relative to the vector of frequencies Y where x is a vector that defines the x-axis positions on which the bars are to be located.*
bar3(...,width)	*Creates a 3D bar graph with the specified bar width. By default, the width is 0.8, and a width of 1 causes the bars to touch.*
bar3(...,'style')	*Creates a 3D bar graph with the specified style of bars. The possible styles are 'detached' (default), 'grouped' (grouped vertical bars) and 'stacked' (stacked bars, one for each row in Y).*
bar3(...,color)	*Creates a 3D bar graph where the bars are all of the specified color (r = red, g = green, b = blue, c = cyan, m = magenta, y = yellow, k = black and w = white).*
comet3(z) **comet3(x, y, z)**	*Creates a 3D comet plot animation of the vector z or of the parametric space curve (x(t),y(t),z(t)).*

```
>> t = -pi:pi/500:pi;comet3(sin(5*t),cos(3*t),t)
```

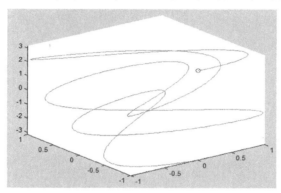

(*continued*)

[X, Y, Z] = cylinder	*Returns the coordinates of a cylinder centered at the origin of radius 1 and (z-axis aligned) length 1 and with 20 equally spaced points around its circumference.*
[X, Y, Z] = cylinder (r (t))	*Returns the coordinates of the cylinder generated by the curve r.*
[X, Y, Z] = cylinder (r (t), n)	*Returns the coordinates of the cylinder generated by the curve r with n points on the circumference (n = 20 by default).*
cylinder(...)	*The cylinders created above can be plotted using the command surf or with the command cylinder(...).*

```
>> t = 0:pi/10:2*pi;
[X,Y,Z] = cylinder(2+cos(t));
surf(X,Y,Z)
```

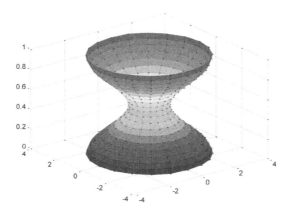

| **sphere** | *Plots the unit sphere with center the origin using 20 × 20 faces.* |
| **sphere(n)** | *Plots a unit sphere using n × n faces.* |

```
>> sphere(100)
```

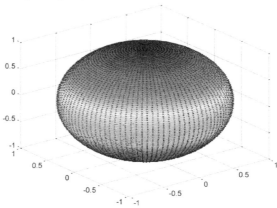

(continued)

106

[X, Y, Z] = sphere(n)	*Gives the coordinates of the sphere in three $(n + 1) \times (n + 1)$ arrays.*
slice(V,sx,sy,sz) **slice(X,Y,Z,V,sx,sy,sz)** **slice(V,XI,YI,ZI)** **slice(X,Y,Z,V,XI,YI,ZI)** **slice(...,'method')**	*Draws slices along the x, y, z directions in the volume V at the points in the vectors sx, sy, and sz. V is an m-by-n-by-p volume array containing data values at the default location X = 1:n, Y = 1:m, Z =1:p. Each element in the vectors sx, sy, and sz defines a slice plane in the x-, y-, or z-axis direction.*

Draws slices of the volume V where X, Y, and Z are monotonic orthogonally spaced three-dimensional arrays specifying the coordinates for V. The color at each point is determined by 3-D interpolation into the volume V.

Draws data in the volume V for the slices defined by matrices XI, YI, and ZI which define a surface, and the volume is evaluated at the surface points. XI, YI, and ZI must all be the same size.

Draws slices through the volume V along the surface defined by the arrays XI, YI, ZI.

Specifies the interpolation method. The options are 'linear', 'cubic', or 'nearest'.

```
>> [x, y, z] = meshgrid(-2:.2:2,-2:.25:2,-2:.16:2);
v = x. * exp(-x.^2-y.^2-z.^2);
slice(x,y,z,v,[-1.2,.8,2],2,[-2,0])
```

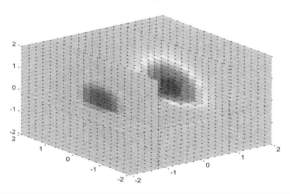

(*continued*)

stem3(Z)	*Plots Z as a sequence of vertical stems with bases on the xy-plane. The base*
stem3(X,Y,Z)	*positions are automatically generated.*
stem3(…,'fill')	*Plots the sequence Z as vertical stems with xy-plane base positions specified by X and Y.*
stem3(…,S)	*Fills the circles at the tips of the stems with color.*
	Creates a 3D stem plot with line style, marker and colour specifications S.

```
>> X = linspace (0,1,10);
Y = X / 2;
Z = sin (X) + cos (Y);
stem3(X,Y,Z,'fill')
```

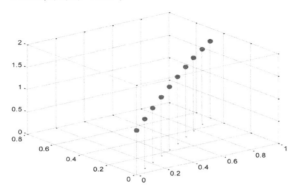

Specialized Graphics

MATLAB provides commands to create various plots and charts (filled areas, comet, contour, mesh, surface and scatter plots, Pareto charts, stairstep graphs). You can also modify axes specifications, and there is an easy to use function plotter. The following table presents the syntax of these commands.

area(Y)	*Creates an area graph displaying the elements of the vector Y as one or more*
area(X, Y)	*curves, filling the area beneath the curve.*
area(…,ymin)	*Identical to plot(X,Y), except the area between 0 and Y is filled.*
	Specifies the base value for the area fill (default 0).

```
>> Y = [1, 5, 3; 3, 2, 7; 1, 5, 3; 2, 6, 1]; area(Y)
```

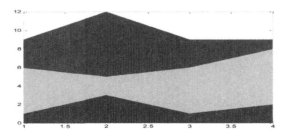

(continued)

box on, box off	*Displays/does not display the boundary of the current axes.*
comet(y)	*Creates an animated comet graph of the vectory y.*
comet(x, y)	*Plots the comet graph of the vector y versus the vector x.*

```
>> t = - pi:pi/200:pi;comet(t,tan(sin(t))-sin(tan(t)))
```

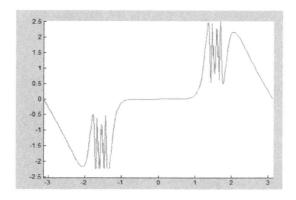

ezcontour(f)	*Creates a contour plot of f(x,y) in the domain [-2π, 2π] × [-2π, 2π].*
ezcontour(f, domain)	*Creates a contour plot of f(x,y) in the given domain.*
ezcontour(...,n)	*Creates a contour plot of f(x,y) over an n × n grid.*

```
>> ezcontour ('sqrt(x^2 + y^2)')
```

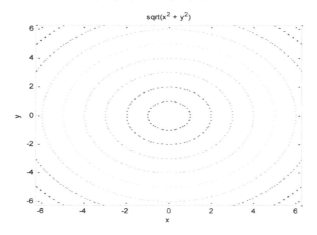

(continued)

ezcontourf(f)	*Creates a filled contour plot of f(x,y) in the domain [-2π, 2π] × [-2π, 2π].*
ezcontourf(f, domain)	*Creates a filled contour plot of f(x,y) in the given domain.*
ezcontourf(…,n)	*Creates a filled contour plot of f(x,y) over an n × n grid.*

```
>> ezcontourf ('sqrt(x^2 + y^2)')
```

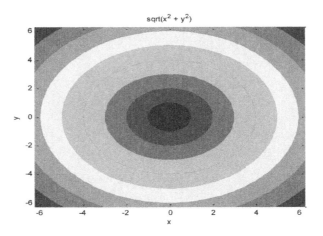

ezmesh(f)	*Creates a mesh plot of f(x,y) over the domain [-2π, 2π] × [-2π, 2π].*
ezmesh(f,domain)	*Creates a mesh plot of f(x,y) over the given domain.*
ezmesh(…,n)	*Creates a mesh plot of f(x,y) using an n × n grid.*
ezmesh(x, y, z)	*Creates a mesh plot of the parametric surface x = x(t,u), y = y(t,u), z = z(t,u),*
ezmesh(x, y, z, domain)	*t,u∈ [-2π, 2π].*
ezmesh(…, 'circ')	*Creates a mesh plot of the parametric surface x = x(t,u), y = y(t,u), z = z(t,u), t,u∈ domain.*
	Creates a mesh plot over a disc centered on the domain.

```
>> ezmesh ('sqrt(x^2 + y^2)')
```

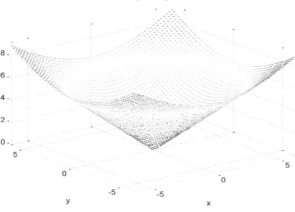

(continued)

ezmeshc(f)
ezmeshc(f, domain)
ezmeshc(...,n)
ezmeshc(x, y, z)
ezmeshc(x, y, z, domain)
ezmeshc(..., 'circ')

Creates a combination of mesh and contour graphs.

```
>> ezmeshc ('sqrt(x^2 + y^2)')
```

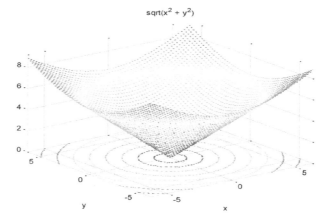

ezsurf(f)
ezsurf(f, domain)
ezsurf(...,n)
ezsurf(x, y, z)
ezsurf(x, y, z, domain)
ezsurf(..., 'circ')

Creates a colored surface plot.

```
>> ezsurf ('sqrt(x^2 + y^2)')
```

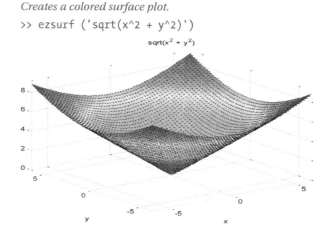

(continued)

111

ezsurfc(f)	*Creates a combination of surface and contour plots.*
ezsurfc(f, domain)	`>> ezsurfc ('sqrt(x^2 + y^2)')`
ezsurfc(...,n)	
ezsurfc(x, y, z)	
ezsurfc(x, y, z, domain)	
ezsurfc(..., 'circ')	

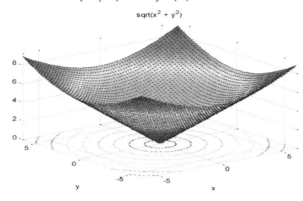

ezplot3(x, y, z)	*Plots the 3D parametric curve $x = x(t)$, (t) $y = y$, $z = z(t)$ $t \in [-2\pi, 2\pi]$.*
ezplot3(x, y, z, domain)	*Plots the 3D parametric curve $x = x(t)$, (t) $y = y$, $z = z(t)$ $t \in domain$.*
ezplot3(..., 'animate')	*Creates a 3D animation of a parametric curve.*
	`>> ezplot3('cos(t)','t.*sin(t)','sqrt(t)')`

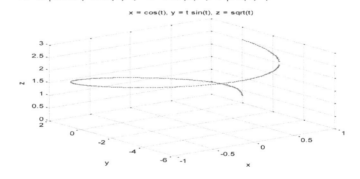

ezpolar(f)	*Graphs the polar curve $r = f(c)$ with $c \in [0, 2\pi]$.*
ezpolar(f, [a, b])	*Graphs the polar curve $r = f(c)$ with $c \in [a, b]$.*
	`ezpolar ('sin(2*t). * cos(3*t)', [0 pi])`

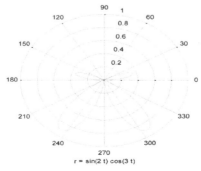

(continued)

pareto(Y)

Creates a Pareto chart relative to the vector of frequencies Y.

pareto(X,Y)

Creates a Pareto chart relative to the vector of frequencies Y whose elements are given by the vector X.

```
>> lines_of_code = [200 120 555 608 1024 101 57 687];
coders = ...
{'Fred', 'Ginger', 'Norman', 'Max', 'Julie', 'Wally', 'Heidi', 'Pat'};
Pareto (lines_of_code, coders)
title ('lines of code by programmer')
```

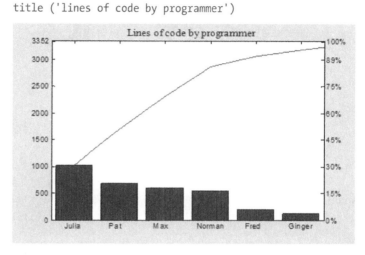

pie.3 (X)

Creates a 3D pie chart for frequencies X.

pie.3(X, explode)

Creates a detached 3D pie chart.

```
>> ft3 ([2 4 3 5], [0 1 1 0], {'North', 'South', 'East', 'West'})
```

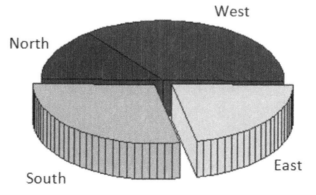

(*continued*)

plotmatrix(X,Y)	*Creates a scatter plot of the columns of X against the columns of Y.*

>> x = randn (50.3); y = x * [- 1 2 1; 2 0 1; 1-2-3;]';plotmatrix (y)

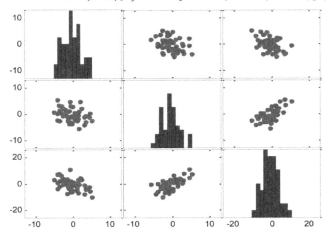

stairs(Y)	*Draws a stairstep graph of the elements of Y.*
stairs(X,Y)	*Draws a stairstep graph of the elements of Y at the locations specified by X.*
stairs(…,linespec)	*In addition specifies line style, marker symbol and color.*

>> x = linspace(-2*pi,2*pi,40);stairs(x,sin(x))

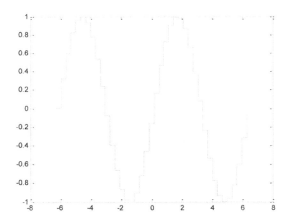

scatter(X,Y,S,C)	*Creates a scatter plot, displaying circles at the locations specified by X and Y.*
scatter(X,Y)	*S specifies the circle size and C the color. The circles can be filled and different*
scatter(X,Y,S)	*markers can be specified.*
scatter(…, marker)	
scatter(…, 'filled')	

(continued)

scatter3(X,Y,Z,S,C)
scatter3(X,Y,Z)
scatter3(X,Y,Z,S)
scatter3(...,marker)
scatter(...,'filled')

Creates a 3D scatter plot determined by the vectors X, Y, Z. Colors and markers can be specified.

```
>> x=(0:0.1:4);
>> scatter(x,cos(x))
```

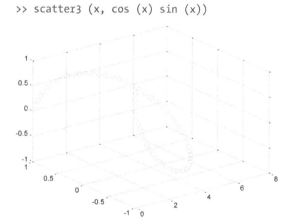

```
>> x=(0:0.1:2*pi);
>> scatter3 (x, cos (x) sin (x))
```

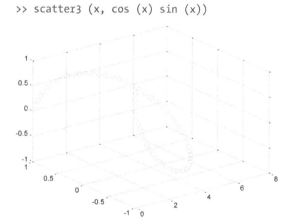

2D and 3D Graphics Options

MATLAB includes many different commands which enable graphics handling, including titles, legends and axis labels, addition of text to plots, and adjustment of coloring and shading. The most important commands are summarized in the following table.

title('text')	*Adds a title to the top of the current axes.*
xlabel('text')	*Adds an x-axis label.*
ylabel('text')	*Adds a y-axis label.*
zlabel('text')	*Adds a z-axis label.*
clabel(C,h)	*Labels contour lines of a contour plot with a '+', rotating the labels so they are positioned on the inside of the contour lines.*
clabel(C,h,v)	*Labels contour lines of a contour plot only for the levels given by the vector v, rotating the labels so they are positioned on the inside of the contour lines.*
datetick(axis)	*Creates date formatted tick labels for the specified axis ('x', 'y' or 'z').*
datetick(axis, date)	*Creates date formatted tick labels for the specified axis ('x', 'y' or 'z') with the given date format (an integer between 1 and 28).*
legend('string1','string2',...)	*Displays a legend in the current axes using the specified strings to label each set of data.*
legend(h,'string1','string2',...)	*Displays a legend on the plot containing the objects identified by the vector h and uses the specified strings to label the corresponding graphics object.*
legend('off'),	*Deletes the current axes legend.*
text(x, y, 'text')	*Places the given text at the point (x, y) within a 2D plot.*
text(x, y, z, 'text')	*Places the given text at the point (x, y, z) in a 3D plot.*
gtext('text')	*Allows you place text at a mouse-selected point in a 2D plot.*
grid	*Adds grid lines to 2D and 3D plots. Grid on adds major grid lines to the axes, grid off removes all grid lines from the current axes. The command grid toggles the visibility of the major grid lines.*
hold	*Controls whether the current graph is cleared when you make subsequent calls to plotting functions (the default), or adds a new graph to the current graph, maintaining the existing graph with all its properties. The command hold on retains the current graph and adds another graph to it. The command hold off resets to default properties before drawing a new graph.*
axis([xmin, xmax, ymin, ymax, zmin, zmax])	*Sets the axes limits.*
axis('auto')	*Computes the axes limits automatically (xmin = min (x), xmax = max(x)).*
axis(axis)	*Freezes the scaling at the current limits, so that if hold is on, subsequent plots use the same limits.*
V = axis	*Returns a row vector V containing scaling factors for the x-, y-, and z-axis. V has four or six components depending on whether the plot is 2D or 3D, respectively.*
axis('xy')	*Uses Cartesian coordinates with the origin at the bottom left of the graph.*
axis('tight')	*Sets the axis limits to the range of the data.*

(continued)

axis('ij')	*Places the origin at the top left of the graph.*
axis('square')	*Makes the current axes region a square (or a cube when three-dimensional).*
axis('equal')	*Uses the same scaling factor for both axes.*
axis('normal')	*Removes the square and equal options.*
axis('off')	*Turns off all axis lines, tick marks, and labels., keeping the title of the graph and any gtext text.*
axis('on')	*Turns on all axis lines, tick marks, and labels.*
subplot(m, n, p)	*Divides the current figure into an m×n grid and creates axes in the grid position specified by p. The grids are numbered by row, so that the first grid is the first column of the first row, the second grid is the second column of the first row, and so on.*
plotyy(X1,Y1,X2,Y2) **plotyy(X1,Y1,X2,Y2,)** **'function')** **plotyy(X1,Y1,X2,Y2;'function1', 'function2')**	*Plots X1 versus Y1 with y-axis labeling on the left and plots X2 versus Y2 with y-axis labeling on the right.* *Same as the previous command, but using the specified plotting function (plot, loglog, semilogx, semilogy, stem or any acceptable function h = function(x,y)) to plot the graph.* *Uses function1(X1,Y1) to plot the data for the left axis and function2(X2,Y2) to plot the data for the right axis.*
axis([xmin, xmax, ymin, ymax, zmin, zmax])	*Sets the x-, y-, and z-axis limits. Also accepts the options 'ij', 'square', 'equal', etc, identical to the equivalent two-dimensional command.*
view([x, y, z])	*Sets the viewing direction to the Cartesian coordinates x, y, and z.*
view([az, el])	*Sets the viewing angle for a three-dimensional plot. The azimuth, az, is the horizontal rotation about the z-axis as measured in degrees from the negative y-axis. Positive values indicate counterclockwise rotation of the viewpoint. el is the vertical elevation of the viewpoint in degrees. Positive values of elevation correspond to moving above the object; negative values correspond to moving below the object.*
hidden	*Hidden line removal draws only those lines that are not obscured by other objects in a 3-D view. The command hidden on hides such obscured lines while hidden off shows them.*
shading	*Controls the type of shading of a surface created with the commands surf, mesh, pcolor, fill and fill3. The option shading flat gives a smooth shading, shading interp gives a dense shadow and shading faceted (default) yields a standard shading.*
colormap(M)	*Sets the colormap to the matrix. M must have three columns and only contain values between 0 and 1. It can also be a matrix whose rows are vectors of RGB type [r g b]. There are some pre-defined arrays M, which are as follows: jet (p), HSV (p), hot (p), cool (p), spring (p), summer (p), autumn (p), winter (p), gray (p), bone (p), copper (p), pink (p), lines (p). All arrays have 3 columns and p rows. For example, the syntax colormap (hot (8)) sets hot (8) as the current colormap.*
brighten(p)	*Adjust the brightness of the figure. If $0 < p < 1$, the figure will be brighter, and if $-1 < p < 0$ the figure will be darker.*

(continued)

image(A)	*Creates an image graphics object by interpreting each element in a matrix as an index into the figure's colormap or directly as RGB values, depending on the data specified.*
pcolor(A)	*Produces a pseudocolor plot, i.e. a rectangular array of cells with colors determined by A. The elements of A are linearly mapped to an index into the current colormap.*
caxis([cmin, cmax])	*Sets the color limits to the specified minimum and maximum values. Data values less than cmin or greater than cmax map to cmin and cmax, respectively. Values between cmin and cmax linearly map to the current colormap.*
h = figure	*Creates a figure graphics object with name h.*
figure(h)	*Makes the figure identified by h the current figure, makes it visible, and attempts to raise it above all other figures on the screen. The current figure is the target for graphics output.*
	The command close(h) deletes the figure identified by h. The command whitebg(h) complements all the colors of the figure h. The clf command closes the current figure. The command graymon sets defaults for graphics properties to produce more legible displays for grayscale monitors. The refresh command redraws the figure.
e = axes	*Creates axes objects named e.*
axes(e)	*Makes the existing axes e the current axes and brings the figure containing it into focus. The command gca returns the name of the current axes. The command cla deletes all objects related to the current axes.*
l = line(x,y) or **l = line (x, y, z)**	*Creates, as an object of name l, the line joining the points X, Y in the plane or the points X, Y, Z in space.*
p = (X, Y, C) patch or **patch(X,Y,Z,C)**	*Creates an opaque polygonal area p that is defined by the set of points (X, Y) in the plane or (X, Y, Z) in space, and whose color is given by C.*
s = surface(X,Y,Z,C)	*Creates parametric surface s defined by X, Y and Z and whose color is given by C.*
i = image (C)	*Creates an image i from the matrix C. Each element of C specifies the color of a rectangular segment in the image.*
t = text (x, y, 'string') or **t = text (x, y, z, 'string')**	*Creates the text t defined by the chain, located at the point (x, y) in the plane, or at the point (x, y, z) in space.*
set (h, 'property1', **'property2',...)**	*Sets the named properties for the object h (gca for limits of axes), gcf, gco, gcbo, gcbd, colors, etc.*
get (h, 'property')	*Returns the current value of the given property of the object h.*
object = gco	*Returns the name of the current object.*
rotate(h, v,α,[p, q, r])	*Rotates the object h by an angle a about an axis of rotation described by the vector v from the point (p, q, r).*
reset (h)	*Updates all properties assigned to the object h replacing them with their default values.*
delete (h)	*Deletes the object h.*

In addition, the most typical properties of graphics objects in MATLAB are the following:

Object	Properties	Possible values
Figure	Color (background color)	'y', 'm', 'c', 'r', 'g', 'b', 'w', 'k'
	ColorMap (map color)	hot(p), gray(p), pink(p), ...
	Position (figure position)	[left, bottom, width, height]
	Name (figure name)	string name
	MinColorMap (min. color no.)	minimum number of colors for map
	NextPlot (graph. mode following.)	new, add, replace
	NumberTitle (no. in the figure title)	on, off
	Units (units of measurement)	pixels, inches, centimeters, points
	Resize (size figure with mouse)	on (can be changed), off (cannot be changed)
Axes	Box (box axes)	on, off
	Color (color of the axes)	'y', ', 'c', 'r', 'g', 'b', 'w', 'k'
	P:System.Windows.Forms.DataGrid.GridLineStyle (line for mesh)	'-', '--', ':', '-.'
	Position (origin position)	[left, bottom, width, height]
	TickLength (distance between marks)	a numeric value
	TickDir (direction of marks)	in, out
	Units (units of measurement)	pixels, inches, centimeters, points
	View (view)	[azimuth, elevation]
	FontAngle (angle of source)	normal, italic, oblique
	FontName (name of source)	the name of the source text
	FontSize (font size)	numeric value
	T:System.Windows.FontWeight (weight)	light, normal, demi, bold
	DrawMode property (drawing mode)	normal, fast
	Xcolor, Ycolor, Zcolor (axes color)	[min, max]
	XDir, Jdir, ZDir (axes direction)	normal (increasing from left to right), reverse
	XGrid, YGrid, Zgrid (grids)	on, off
	XLabel, YLabel, Zlabel (tags)	string containing the text of labels
	XLim, YLim, ZLim (limit values)	[min, max] (range of variation)
	XScale, YScale, ZScale (scales)	linear, log (log)
	XTick,YTick,ZTick (marks)	[m1,m2,...] (position of marks on axis)

(continued)

Line	*Color (color of the line)*	*'y', 'm', 'c', 'r', 'g', 'b', 'w', 'k'*
	LineStyle (line style)	*'-', '--', ':', '-.', '+', '*', '.', 'x'*
	LineWidth (line width)	*numeric value*
	Visible (visible line or not displayed.)	*on, off*
	Xdata, Ydata, Zdata (coordinates.)	*set of coordinates of the line*
Text	*Color (text color)*	*'y', 'm', 'c', 'r', 'g', 'b', 'w', 'k'*
	FontAngle (angle of source)	*normal, italic, oblique*
	FontName (name of source)	*the name of the source text*
	FontSize (font size)	*numeric value*
	T:System.Windows.FontWeight (weight)	*light, normal, demi, bold*
	HorizontalAlignment (hor. setting.)	*left, center, right*
	VerticalAlignment (adjust to vert.)	*top, cap, middle, baseline, bottom*
	Position (position on screen)	*[x, y, z] (text coordinates)*
	Rotation (orientation of the text)	*0, ±90, ±180, ±270*
	Units (units of measurement)	*pixels, inches, centimeters, points*
	String (text string)	*the text string*
Surface	*CDATA (color of each point)*	*color matrix*
	Edgecolor (color grids)	*'y','m',..., none, flat, interp*
	Facecolor (color of the faces)	*'y','m',..., none, flat, interp*
	LineStyle (line style)	*'-', '--', ':', '-.', '+', '*', '.', 'x'*
	LineWidth (line width)	*numeric value*
	MeshStyle (lines in rows and col.)	*row, Columbia, both*
	Visible (visible line or not displayed.)	*on, off*
	Xdata, Ydata, Zdata (coordinates)	*set of coordinates of the surface*
Patch	*CDATA (color of each point)*	*color matrix*
	Edgecolor (color of the axes)	*'y','m',..., none, flat, interp*
	Facecolor (color of the faces)	*'y','m',..., none, flat, interp*
	LineWidth (line width)	*numeric value*
	Visible (visible line or not displayed.)	*on, off*
	Xdata, Ydata, Zdata (coordinates)	*set of coordinates of the surface*
Image	*CDATA (color of each point)*	*color matrix*
	Xdata, Ydata (coordinates)	*set of coordinates of the image*

Here are some illustrative examples.

```
>> x=linspace(0,2,30);
y=sin(x.^2);
plot(x,y)
text(1,0.8, 'y=sin(x^2)')
hold on
z=log(sqrt(x));
plot(x,z)
text(1,-0.1, 'y=log(sqrt(x))')
xlabel('x-axis');
ylabel('y-axis');
title(Sinoidal and logarithmic graphs');
```

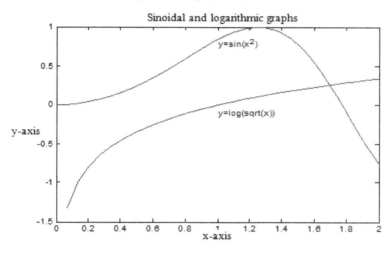

```
>> subplot(2,2,1);
ezplot('sin(x)',[-2*pi 2*pi])
subplot(2,2,2);
ezplot('cos(x)',[-2*pi 2*pi])
subplot(2,2,3);
ezplot('csc(x)',[-2*pi 2*pi])
subplot(2,2,4);
ezplot('sec(x)',[-2*pi 2*pi])
```

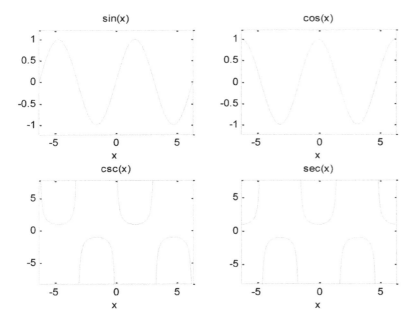

```
>> [X, Y] = meshgrid(-2:0.05:2);
Z = X ^ 2 - Y. ^ 2;
subplot(2,2,1)
surf(X,Y,Z)
subplot(2,2,2)
surf(X,Y,Z),view(-90,0)
subplot(2,2,3)
surf(X,Y,Z),view(60,30)
subplot(2,2,4)
surf(X,Y,Z), view (- 10, 30)
```

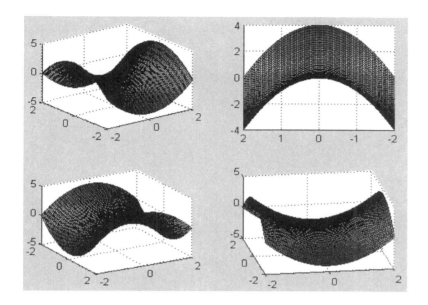

```
>> [X,Y]=meshgrid(-2:0.05:2);
Z=X.^2-Y.^2;
surf(X,Y,Z),shading interp,brighten(0.75),colormap(gray(5))
```

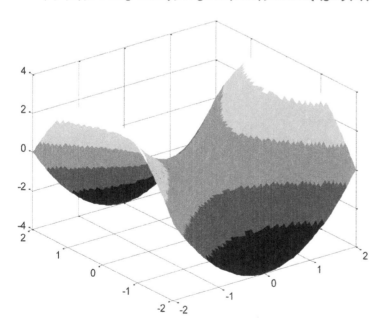

EXERCISE 3-1

Represent the surface defined by the equation:

$$f(x,y) = \frac{(x-1)^2 y^2}{(x-1)^2 + y^2}$$

```
>> [x,y]=meshgrid(0:0.05:2,-2:0.05:2);
>> z=y.^2.*(x-1).^2./(y.^2+(x-1).^2);
>> mesh(x,y,z),view([-23,30])
```

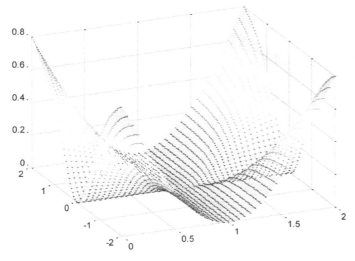

We could also have represented the surface in the following form:

```
>> ezsurf('y^2*(x-1)^2/(y^2+(x-1)^2)')
```

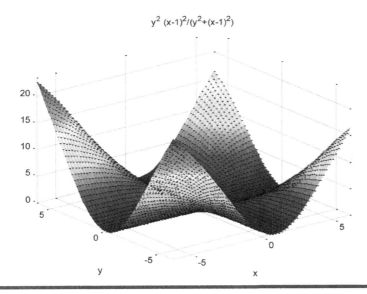

EXERCISE 3-2

Let the function f:R^2→ R be defined by:

$$f(x,y) = \frac{(1-\cos(x))\sin(y)}{x^3 + y^3}$$

Represent it graphically in a neighborhood of (0,0).

```
>> [x,y]=meshgrid(-1/100:0.0009:1/100,-1/100:0.0009:1/100);
>> z=(1-cos(x)).*sin(y)./(x.^3+y.^3);
>> surf(x,y,z)
>> view([50,-15])
```

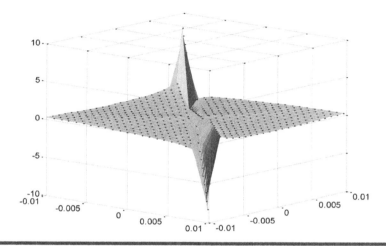

EXERCISE 3-3

Plot the following two curves, given in polar coordinates, next to each other:

$$r = \sqrt{\cos(2a)} \quad and \quad r = \sin(2a).$$

Also find the intersection of the two curves.

```
>> a=0:.1:2*pi;
>> subplot(1,2,1)
>> r=sqrt(cos(2*a));
>> polar(a,r)
>> title('r = sqrt(cos(2a))')
>> subplot (1,2,2)
>> r = sin(2*a);
>> polar (a, r)
>> title('r = sin(2a)')
```

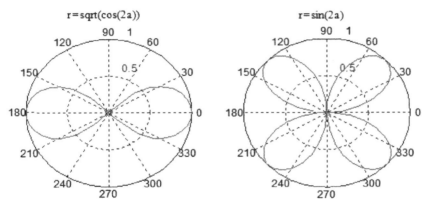

To find the intersection of the two curves, we draw them both on the same axes.

```
>> a = 0:. 1:2 * pi;
>> r=sqrt(cos(2*a));
>> polar(a,r)
>> hold on;
>> r=sin(2*a);
>> polar(a,r)
```

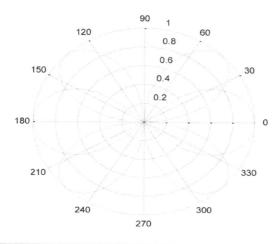

EXERCISE 3-4

Represent the surface generated by rotating the cubic $y = 12x - 9x^2 + 2x^3$ around the OX axis, between the limits $x = 0$ and $x = 5/2$.

The surface of revolution has equation $y^2 + z^2 = (12x - 9x^2 + 2x^3)^2$, and to graph it we use the following parameterization:

$$x = t, \quad y = \cos(u)\left(12t - 9t^2 + 2t^3\right), \quad z = \sin(u)\left(12t - 9t^2 + 2t^3\right).$$

```
>> t=(0:.1:5/2);
>> u=(0:.5:2*pi);
>> x=ones(size(u))'*t;
>> y=cos(u)'*(12*t-9*t.^2+2*t.^3);
>> z=sin(u)'*(12*t-9*t.^2+2*t.^3);
>> surf(x,y,z)
```

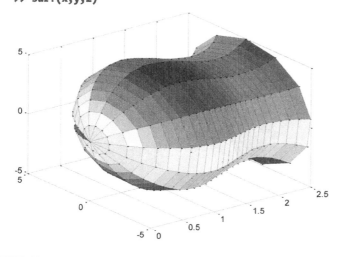

EXERCISE 3-5

Plot the surfaces produced by rotating the ellipse $\dfrac{x^2}{4}+\dfrac{y^2}{9}=1$ around the OX axis and around the OY axis.

We represent the generated figures alongside each other, but only the positive halves of each figure. The equation of the surface of revolution around the OX axis is $y^2 + z^2 = 9(1 - x^2/4)$, and is given parametrically by:

$$x=t, \quad y=3\cos(u)\left(1-4t^2\right)^{\frac{1}{2}}, \quad z=3\sin(u)(1-4t^2)^{1/2}$$

The equation of the surface of revolution around the OY axis is $x^2 + z^2 = 4(1 - y^2/4)$ and has the parametrization:

$$x=3\cos(u)\left(1-9t^2\right)^{\frac{1}{2}}, \quad y=t, \quad z=3\sin(u)\left(1-9t^2\right)^{\frac{1}{2}}.$$

```
>> t=(0:.1:2);
>> u=(0:.5:2*pi);
>> x=ones(size(u))'*t;
>> y=cos(u)'*3*(1-t.^2/4).^(1/2);
>> z=sin(u)'*3*(1-t.^2/4).^(1/2);
>> subplot(1,2,1)
>> surf(x,y,z)
>> subplot(1,2,2)
>> x=cos(u)'*3*(1-t.^2/4).^(1/2);
>> y=ones(size(u))'*t;
>> z=sin(u)'*3*(1-t.^2/4).^(1/2);
>> surf(x,y,z)
```

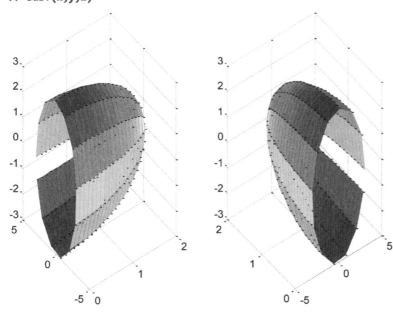

EXERCISE 3-6

Represent the intersection of the paraboloid $x^2 + y^2 = 2\,z$ with the plane $z = 2$.

```
>> [x,y]=meshgrid(-3:.1:3);
>> z=(1/2)*(x.^2+y.^2);
>> mesh(x,y,z)
>> hold on;
>> z=2*ones(size(z));
>> mesh(x,y,z)
>> view(-10,10)
```

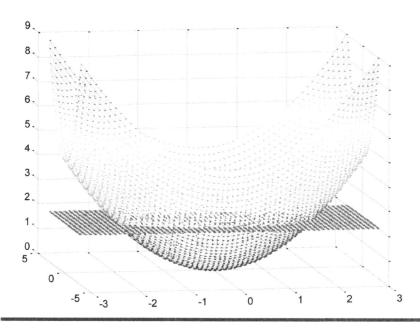

EXERCISE 3-7

Represent the volume in the first octant enclosed between the OXY plane, the plane $z = x + y + 2$ and the cylinder $x^2 + y^2 = 16$.

We graphically represent the enclosed volume using Cartesian coordinates for the plane and parametrizing the cylinder.

```
>> t=(0:.1:2*pi);
>> u=(0:.1:10);
>> x=4*cos(t)'*ones(size(u));
>> y=4*sin(t)'*ones(size(u));
>> z=ones(size(t))'*u;
>> mesh(x,y,z)
>> hold on;
>> [x,y]=meshgrid(-4:.1:4);
>> z=x+y+2;
>> mesh(x,y,z)
>> set(gca,'Box','on');
>> view(15,45)
```

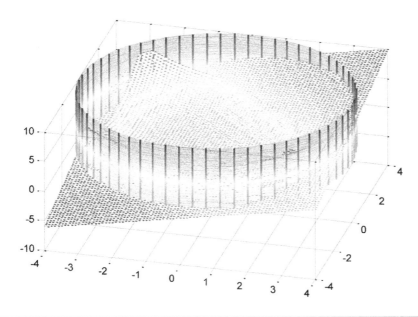

EXERCISE 3-8

Represent the volume bounded by the paraboloid $x^2 + 4y^2 = z$ and laterally by the cylinders $y^2 = x$ and $x^2 = y$.

```
>> [x,y]=meshgrid(-1/2:.02:1/2,-1/4:.01:1/4);
>> z = x ^ 2 + 4 * y. ^ 2;
>> mesh(x,y,z)
>> hold on;
>> y=x.^2;
>> mesh(x,y,z)
>> hold on;
>> x=y.^2;
>> mesh(x,y,z)
>> set(gca,'Box','on')
>> view(-60,40)
```

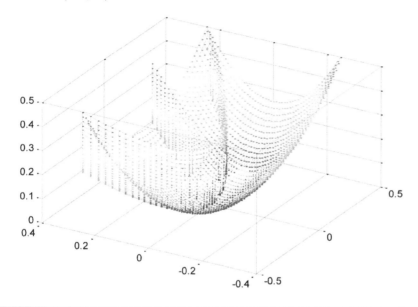

EXERCISE 3-9

Plot the parabolas $y^2 = x$ and $x^2 = y$ on the same axes. Also plot the parabola $y^2 = 4x$ and the straight line $x + y = 3$ on the same axes.

```
>> fplot('[x^2,sqrt(x)]',[0,1.2])
```

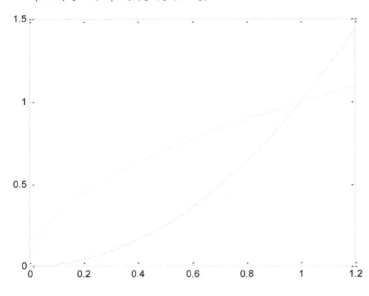

```
>> fplot('[(4*x)^(1/2),3-x]',[0,4,0,4])
```

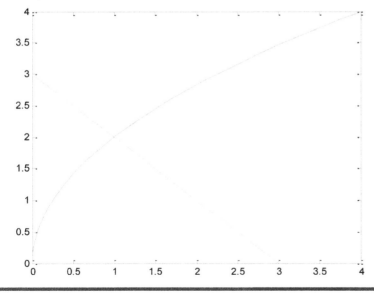

EXERCISE 3-10

Plot the curves defined by the following implicit equations:

$$x^5 - x^2y^2 + y^5 = 0$$

$$x^4 + x^2y - y^5 + y^4 = 0$$

```
>> ezplot('x^5-x^2*y^2+y^5', [-1,1,-1,1])
```

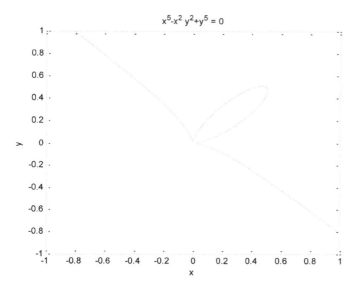

```
>> ezplot('x^4+x^2*y-y^3+y^4', [-1/2,1/2,-1/2,3/2])
```

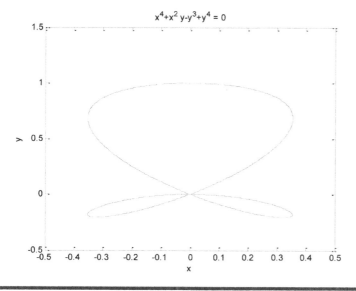

EXERCISE 3-11

Plot the curve given by the following parametric equations:

$$x(t) = t\sin(t)$$

$$y(t) = t\cos(t)$$

```
>> ezplot ('t * sin (t) ',' t * cos (t)')
```

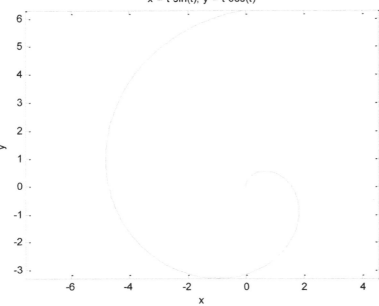

EXERCISE 3-12

Plot the curve given by the following equation in polar coordinates:

$$r = 1 \; \cos(\theta).$$

```
>> ezpolar ('1 - cos (t)')
```

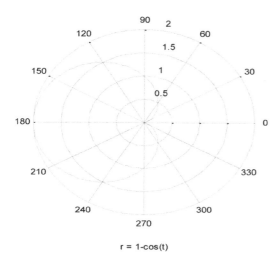

r = 1-cos(t)

EXERCISE 3-13

Plot the space curve defined by the following parametric equations:

$$x = cos\ (t),\quad y = sin\ (t),\quad z = t.$$

```
>> ezplot3('cos(t)','sin(t)','t',[0,6*pi])
```

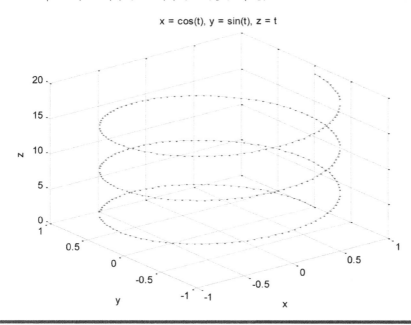

■ ■ ■

CHAPTER 4

Algebraic Expressions, Polynomials, Equations and Systems

Expanding, Simplifying and Factoring Algebraic Expressions

MATLAB incorporates a wide range of commands, including simplification, expansion and factorization, that allow you to work with algebraic expressions. The following table shows the most common commands used when working with algebraic expressions.

---

expand (expr)   *Expands an algebraic expression, presenting the result as a sum of products and powers, applying multiple angle rules for trigonometric expressions and the formal properties of exponential and logarithmic functions. It also decomposes quotients of polynomials into sums of simpler polynomial quotients.*

```
>> syms x y z t a b
>> pretty(expand((x+2)*(x+3)))

 2
x  + 5 x + 6

>> pretty(expand((x+2)/(x+3)))

  x        2
----- + -----
x + 3   x + 3

>> pretty(expand(cos(x+y)))

cos(x) cos(y) - sin(x) sin(y)
```

(continued)

factor (expr)	*The reverse operation of expand. Writes an algebraic expression as a product of factors.*

```
>> syms x y
>> pretty(factor(6*x^2+18*x-24))

6 (x + 4) (x - 1)

>> pretty (factor ((x^3-y^3)/(x^4-y^4)))

 2        2
x + x y + y
-----------------
        2    2
(x + y) (x + y )

>> pretty(factor(x^3+y^3))

        2        2
(x + y) (x - x y + y )
```

simplify (expr)	*Simplifies an algebraic expression as much as possible.*

```
>> syms x y b c
>> simplify (sin (x) ^ 2 + cos (x) ^ 2) * 2

ans =

2

>> simplify (log (exp (a+log (exp (c)))))

ans =

log (exp(a + c))
```

(continued)

simple (expr)   *Searches for the simplest form of an algebraic expression.*

```
>> syms a positive;
f = (1/a^3 + 6/a^2 + 12/a + 8)^(1/3);
>> simplify(f)

ans =

(8*a^3 + 12*a^2 + 6*a + 1)^(1/3)/a

>> simple(f)

simplify:

(2*a + 1)/a

radsimp:

(12/a + 6/a^2 + 1/a^3 + 8)^(1/3)

simplify(100):

1/a + 2

combine(sincos):

(12/a + 6/a^2 + 1/a^3 + 8)^(1/3)

combine(sinhcosh):

(12/a + 6/a^2 + 1/a^3 + 8)^(1/3)

combine(ln):

(12/a + 6/a^2 + 1/a^3 + 8)^(1/3)

factor:

(12/a + 6/a^2 + 1/a^3 + 8)^(1/3)

expand:

(12/a + 6/a^2 + 1/a^3 + 8)^(1/3)
```

(continued)

```
combine:

(12/a + 6/a^2 + 1/a^3 + 8)^(1/3)

rewrite(exp):

(12/a + 6/a^2 + 1/a^3 + 8)^(1/3)

rewrite(sincos):

(12/a + 6/a^2 + 1/a^3 + 8)^(1/3)

rewrite(sinhcosh):

(12/a + 6/a^2 + 1/a^3 + 8)^(1/3)

rewrite(tan):

(12/a + 6/a ^ 2 + 1/a ^ 3 + 8) ^(1/3)

mwcos2sin:

(12/a + 6/a ^ 2 + 1/a ^ 3 + 8) ^(1/3)

collect(a):

(12/a + 6/a^2 + 1/a^3 + 8)^(1/3)

ans =

1/a + 2

>> g=simple(f)

g =

1/a + 2
```

(continued)

collect (expr)	*Groups terms of the expression together into powers of its variables.*

```
>> syms x;
f = x*(x*(x - 6) + 11) - 6;
>> collect(f)

ans =

x^3 - 6*x^2 + 11*x - 6

>> f = (1+x)*t + x*t;
>> collect(f)

ans =

(2*t)*x + t
```

Horner (expr)	*Factors the expression in Horner form.*

```
>> syms x;
f = x^3 - 6*x^2 + 11*x - 6;
>> horner(f)

ans =

x*(x*(x - 6) + 11) - 6
```

Polynomials

MATLAB implements specific commands for working with polynomials, such as finding their roots, differentiation and interpolation. The following table shows the syntax and examples of the most important of these commands.

poly2sym (vector)	*Converts a vector of coefficients into the corresponding symbolic polynomial (from highest to lowest power).*

```
>> poly2sym([3 5 0 8 9])

ans =

3*x^4 + 5*x^3 + 8*x + 9
```

poly2sym(vector,'v')	*Converts a vector of coefficients into the corresponding symbolic polynomial in v (from highest to lowest power).*

```
>> poly2sym([3 5 0 8 9],'z')

ans =

3*z^4 + 5*z^3 + 8*z + 9
```

(continued)

sym2poli (polynomial)   *Converts a symbolic polynomial into a vector of coefficients (the coefficient are given in decreasing order of power).*

```
>> syms x
>> sym2poly(x^5-3*x^4+2*x^2-7*x+12)

ans =

1    -3    0    2    -7    12
```

q=conv(u,v)   *Gives the coefficients of the polynomial product of two polynomials whose coefficients are given by the vectors u and v.*

```
>> u=[3 -1 4 2];v=[2 1 4 6 8 3];
>> p=conv(u,v)

p =

6    1    19    22    36    33    41    28    6

>> poly2sym(p)

ans =

6*x^8 + x^7 + 19*x^6 + 22*x^5 + 36*x^4 + 33*x^3 + 41*x^2 + 28*x + 6
```

[q, r] = deconv(v,u)   *Gives the polynomial quotient and remainder of the division between polynomials u and v, so that v = conv (u, q) + r.*

```
>> [q,r]=deconv(v,u)

q =

0.6667    0.5556    0.6296

r =

0    0    0    3.0741    4.3704    1.7407

>> poly2sym(q)

ans =

(2*x^2)/3 + (5*x)/9 + 17/27

>> poly2sym(r)

ans =

(83*x^2)/27 + (118*x)/27 + 47/27
```

(continued)

p = poly (r)	*Gives the coefficients of the polynomial p whose roots are specified by the vector r.*

```
>> p=poly(u)

p =

1    -8    17    2    -24

>> poly2sym(p)

ans =

x^4 - 8*x^3 + 17*x^2 + 2*x - 24
```

k = polyder(p)	*Gives the coefficients k of the derivative of the polynomial p.*
k = polyder(a,b)	*Gives the coefficients k of the derivative of the product of polynomials a and b.*
[q,d] = polyder(a,b)	*Gives the numerator q and denominator d of the derivative of a/b*

```
>> polyder([1 -8 17 2 -24])

ans =

4    -24    34    2

>> poly2sym([1 -8 17 2 -24])

ans =

x^4 - 8*x^3 + 17*x^2 + 2*x - 24

>> poly2sym(polyder([1 -8 17 2 -24]))

ans =

4*x^3 - 24*x^2 + 34*x + 2

>> u = [3 - 1 4 2]; v = [2 1 4 6 8 3];
>> k = polyder(u,v)

k =

48    7    114    110    144    99    82    28
```

(*continued*)

```
>> poly2sym(k)

ans =

48*x^7 + 7*x^6 + 114*x^5 + 110*x^4 + 144*x^3 + 99*x^2 + 82*x + 28

>> [q, d] = polyder(u,v)

q =

  -12     3    -30    -10     8    -29    -30     -4

d =

   4     4    17    32    60    76    106    120    100    48     9
```

p = polyfit(x, y, n)	*Finds the polynomial of degree n which is the best fit of the set of points (x, y).*
[p,S] = polyfit(x,y,n)	*Finds the polynomial of degree n which is the best fit of the set of points (x, y) and also returns structure data S of the fit.*
[p, S, u] = polyfit (x, y, n)	*Finds the coefficients of the polynomial in $\hat{x}=(x-m)\big/ s$ which best fits the data,*

and also returns the structure data S and the row vector $u=[m,s]$, where m is the mean and s is the standard deviation of the data x.

```
>> u=[3 -1 4 2];v=[2 1 4 6];
>> p=poly2sym(polyfit(u,v,3))

p =

(53*x^3)/60 - (99*x^2)/20 + (119*x)/30 + 54/5

>> [p,S,u]=polyfit(u,v,3)

p =

   8.9050    1.6333   -11.3053    6.0000

S =

R: [4x4 double]
df: 0
normr: 1.2686e-014

u =

2.0000
2.1602
```

(continued)

y = polyval(p,x)	*Evaluates the polynomial p at x.*
y = polyval(p,x,[ ],u)	*If $u=[m,s]$, evaluates the polynomial p at $\hat{x}=(x-m)\Big/_s$.*
[y, delta] = polyval (p,x,S)	*Uses the optional output structure S generated by polyfit to generate error estimates delta.*
[y, delta] = polyval(p,x,S,u)	*Does the above with $\hat{x}=(x-m)\Big/_s$ in place of x, where u[m,s].*

```
>> p=[2 0 -1 7 9]

p =

2     0    -1     7     9

>> poly2sym(p)

ans =

2*x^4 - x^2 + 7*x + 9

>> polyval(p,10)

ans =

19979
```

Y = polyvalm (p, X)	*For a polynomial p and a matrix X, evaluates p(X) in the matrix sense.*

```
>> X=[1 2 3;4 5 6;7 8 9]

X =

1     2     3
4     5     6
7     8     9

>> p=[2 0 -1 7 9]

p =

2     0    -1     7     9

>> A=polyval(p,X)

A =

17        51        183
533      1269      2607
4811     8193     13113
```

(*continued*)

[r,p,k] = residue(b,a) *Finds the residues, poles and direct term of the rational expansion of b/a.*

$$\frac{b(s)}{a(s)} = \frac{r_1}{s-p_1} + \frac{r_2}{s-p_2} + \cdots + \frac{r_n}{s-p_n} + k(s).$$

[b,a] = residue(r,p,k) *Converts the partial fraction expansion back into a quotient of polynomials.*

```
>> u=[3 -1 4 2];v=[2 1 4 6 8 3];
>> [r,p,k]=residue(v,u)


r =

0.4751 - 0.6032i
0.4751 + 0.6032i
0.0745


p =

0.3705 + 1.2240i
0.3705 - 1.2240i
-0.4076


k =

0.6667    0.5556    0.6296

>> [v,u]=residue(r,p,k)

v =

0.6667    0.3333    1.3333    2.0000    2.6667    1.0000

u =

1.0000    -0.3333    1.3333    0.6667
```

r = roots (c) *Gives the column vector r of the roots of the polynomial with coefficients c.*

```
>> v=[0.6667    0.3333    1.3333    2.0000    2.6667    1.0000];
>> r=roots(v)

r =

0.6662 + 1.4813i
0.6662 - 1.4813i
-0.6662 + 0.8326i
-0.6662 - 0.8326i
-0.5000
```

Polynomial Interpolation

MATLAB implements both algebraic and graphical commands for polynomial interpolation, the most important of which are summarized in the following table.

Yi = interp1 (X, Y, Xi)	*Returns a vector Yi such that (Xi, Yi) is the total set of points found by one-dimensional linear interpolation of the given set of points (X, Y).*
Yi = interp1(Y,Xi)	*Equivalent to interp1(X,Y,Xi) with X = 1: n, where n is the length of Y.*
Yi = interp1(X,Y,Xi, method)	*Performs the interpolation using the given method, which can be nearest (nearest neighbor), linear, cubic (cubic Hermite), v5cubic (MATLAB 5 cubic), spline or pchip (cubic Hermite).*
Yi= interp1(X,Y,Xi, method,ext)	*Additionally specifies a strategy for evaluating points that lie outside the domain of X.*

In the following example, 21 points (x,y) are interpolated depending on the function $y = sin(x)$ for x values equally spaced between 0 and 10.

```
>> x = 0:10; y = sin (x); Xi = 0:.5:10; yi = interp1 (x, y, xi);
points = [xi', yi']

points =

0          0
0.5000     0.4207
1.0000     0.8415
1.5000     0.8754
2.0000     0.9093
2.5000     0.5252
3.0000     0.1411
3.5000    -0.3078
4.0000    -0.7568
4.5000    -0.8579
5.0000    -0.9589
5.5000    -0.6192
6.0000    -0.2794
6.5000     0.1888
7.0000     0.6570
7.5000     0.8232
8.0000     0.9894
8.5000     0.7007
9.0000     0.4121
9.5000    -0.0660
10.0000   -0.5440
```

(continued)

We can represent the points in the following form:

```
plot(x,y,'o',xi,yi)
```

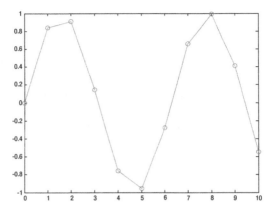

Zi = interp2(X,Y,Z,Xi,Yi)	*Returns a vector Zi such that (Xi, Yi, Zi) is the set of points found by two-dimensional linear interpolation of the set of given points (X, Y, Z).*
Zi = interp2(Z,Xi,Yi)	*Equivalent to the above with X = 1: n and Y = 1:m where (n, m) = size(Z).*
Zi = interp2(Z,n)	*Returns the interpolated values on a refined grid formed by repeatedly dividing the intervals n times in each dimension.*
Zi = interp2(X,Y,Z,Xi,Yi, *method*)	*In addition specifies the method of interpolation. Possible methods are nearest (nearest neighbor), linear, cubic (cubic Hermite) and spline interpolation.*

In the following example we consider a set of years, years of service and wages and try to find by interpolation the salary earned in 1975 by an employee with 15 years of service.

```
>> years = 10:1950:1990;
service = 10:10:30;
wages = [150.697 199.592 187.625
179.323 195.072 250.287
203.212 179.092 322.767
226.505 153.706 426.730
249.633 120.281 598.243];
w = interp2(service,years,wages,15,1975)

w =

190.6288
```

(*continued*)

vi = interp3(X,Y,Z,V,Xi,Yi,Zi)	*Returns interpolated values of a function of three variables at specific query points using linear interpolation. The results always pass through the original sampling of the function. X, Y, and Z contain the coordinates of the sample points. V contains the corresponding function values at each sample point. Xi, Yi, and Zi contain the coordinates of the query points.*
vi = interp3(V, Xi, Yi, Zi)	*Equivalent to the above with* $X = 1:n, Y = 1:m, Z = 1:p$ *where* $(n,m,p) = size(V)$.
vi = interp3(V,n)	*Returns the interpolated values on a refined grid formed by repeatedly dividing the intervals n times in each dimension.*
	Performs the interpolation using the specified method.
vi = interp3(..., method)	

The following example calculates and represents interpolated values of the MATLAB function *flow* by taking several slices through the data and displaying the interpolated data on each slice. The three axes are sampled in equal intervals of 0.5, for x between 0.1 and 10 and y and z between -3 and 3.

```
>> [x, y, z, v] = flow (10);
[xi, yi, zi] = meshgrid(.1:.5:10,-3:.5:3,-3:.5:3);
vi = interp3(x,y,z,v,xi,yi,zi);
slice(xi,yi,zi,vi,[6 9.5],2,[-2 .2]), shading flat
```

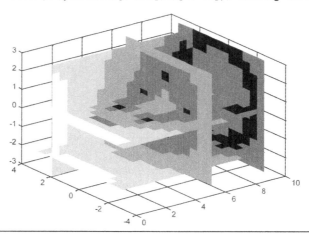

(*continued*)

Y = interpft(X,n)	*One-dimensional interpolation using the FFT method. Gives the vector containing the values of the periodic function X sampled at n equally spaced points. The original vector X is transformed to the Fourier domain via the fast Fourier transform (FFT).*
	Operates along the specified dimension.
y = interpft (x, n, dim)	Below is an example where the original points and the interpolated points using the FFT method are compared.

```
>> y = [0:. 5:2 1.5:-. 5: - 2 - 1.5:. 5:0]; % Equally spaced
points
factor = 5; A factor of 5% Tween
m = length (y) * factor;
x = 1:factor: m;
XI = 1;
Yi = interpft (y, m);
plot(x,y,'o',xi,yi,'*')
Legend ('original data', 'interpolated data')
```

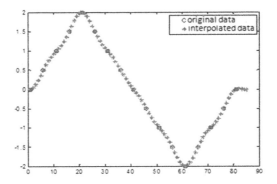

Vi = interpn(X,Y,Z,...V, Xi, Yi, Zi...)	*Returns interpolated values of a function of n variables at specific query points using linear interpolation. The results always pass through the original sampling of the function. X,Y,Z,... contain the coordinates of the sample points. V contains the corresponding function values at each sample point. Xi,Yi,Zi,... contain the coordinates of the query points.*
Vi = interpn (V, Xi, Yi, Zi)	*Equivalent to the above with $X = 1:n, Y = 1:m, Z = 1:p,...$ where $(n,m,p,...) = size(V)$.*
Vi = interpn (V, n)	*Returns the interpolated values on a refined grid formed by repeatedly dividing the intervals n times in each dimension.*
Vi = interpn(...,method)	*Interpolation using the specified method.*
Yi= pchip (X, Y, Xi)	*Returns a vector Yi containing elements corresponding to the elements of Xi and determined by piecewise cubic interpolation within vectors X and Y.*
pp = pchip(X,Y)	*Returns a piecewise polynomial structure for use by ppval.*

(continued)

Yi = spline (X, Y, Xi) ⁻

Uses a cubic spline interpolation to find Yi, the values of the underlying function Y at the values of the interpolant Xi. The simple points are determined by X.

pp = spline(X,Y)

Returns the piecewise polynomial form of the cubic spline interpolant for later use with ppval and the spline utility unmkpp.

In the following example the original points are compared with the interpolated points obtained using the the *pchip* and *spline* methods.

```
>> x = - 3:3;
y = [- 1 - 1 - 1 0 1 1 1];
t = - 3:. 01:3;
plot (x, y, 'o', t, [pchip (x, y, t); spline(x,y,t)])
legend('data','pchip','spline',4)
```

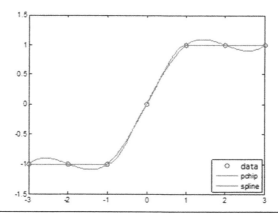

(*continued*)

Zi = griddata(X,Y,Z,Xi,Yi)	*Fits a surface of the form Z = f(X,Y) to the scattered data in the vectors (X,Y,Z). The function interpolates the surface at the query points specified by (Xi,Yi) and returns the interpolated values, Zi. The surface always passes through the data points defined by X and Y. The method of interpolation is linear by default.*
[Xi, Yi, Zi] = griddata(X,Y,Z,Xi,Yi)	*Returns in addition to Zi the vectors Xi and Yi.*
[...] = griddata(...,method)	*Interpolation using the specified method.*

The example below interpolates scattered data over a grid.

```
x = rand (100.1) * 4-2; y = rand (100.1) * 4-2;
z = x.*exp(-x.^2-y.^2);
ti = -2:.25:2;
[xi,yi] = meshgrid(ti,ti);
Zi = griddata(x,y,z,xi,yi);
mesh(xi,yi,zi), hold on, plot3(x,y,z,'o'),
hold off
```

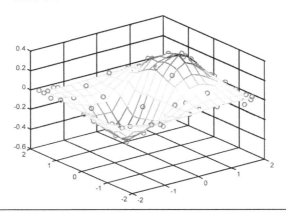

(*continued*)

W = griddata3(X,Y,Z,V,Xi,Yi,Zi)   *Fits a hypersurface of the form V = f(X,Y,Z) to the scattered data in the vectors (X,Y,Z,V). The function interpolates the hypersurface at the query points specified by (Xi,Yi,Zi) and returns the interpolated values, W. The surface always passes through the data points defined by X, Y and Z. The method of interpolation is linear by default.*

W = griddata3(...,'method')   *Interpolation using the specified method.*

Below is an example of fitting a hypersurface to scattered data by interpolation.

```
>>  x = 2*rand(5000,1)-1; y = 2*rand(5000,1)-1;
z = 2*rand(5000,1)-1;
v = x.^2 + y.^2 + z.^2;
d = -0.8:0.05:0.8;
[xi,yi,zi] = meshgrid(d,d,d);
w = griddata3(x,y,z,v,xi,yi,zi);
p = patch(isosurface(xi,yi,zi,w,0.8));
isonormals(xi,yi,zi,w,p);
set(p,'FaceColor','blue','EdgeColor','none');
view(3), axis equal, axis off, camlight, lighting phong
```

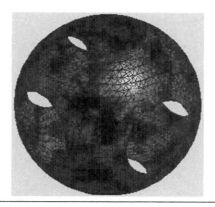

Solving Equations and Systems of Equations

MATLAB includes multiple commands for solving equations and systems of equations. The following sections present the syntax and main features of these methods.

General Methods

Below are the most common MATLAB commands used to solve equations and systems

solve('equation','x')	*Solve the equation in the variable x.*
	The equation $p*\sin(x)=r$ *is solved as follows:*
	`>> solve('p*sin(x) = r')`
	`ans =`
	`asin(r/p)` `pi - asin(r/p)`
syms x; solve (equ (x), x)	*Solve the equation equ* $(x)=0$ *in the variable x.*
	The equation $p*\cos(x)=r$ *is solved as follows:*
	`>> syms x r; solve (p * cos (x) - r, x)`
	`ans =`
	`acos ((8192*r)/1433639)` `-acos ((8192*r)/1433639)`
solve('eq1,eq2,...,eqn', 'x1, x2,...,xn')	*Solves the n simultaneous equations eq1,..., eqn (the solutions are assigned to the variables x1,..., xn)*
	`>> [x, y] = solve('x^2 + x*y + y = 3','x^2-4*x + 3 = 0')`
	`x =`
	`1` `3`
	`y =`
	`1` `-3/2`
syms x1 x2...xn; solve(eq1,eq2,...,eqn, x1, x2,...,xn)	*Solves the n simultaneous equations eq1,..., eqn (the solutions are assigned to the variables x1,..., xn)*
	`>> syms x y; [x, y] = solve(x^2 + x*y + y-3, x^2-4*x + 3)`
	`x =`
	`1` `3`
	`y =`
	`1` `-3/2`

(continued)

X = linsolve (A, B)	*Solves the equation $A * X = B$ where A,B and X are matrices.*
	We solve the system:

$$2x+y+z+t=1$$
$$x+y+z+t=2$$
$$x+y+z+2t=3$$
$$x+y+z+2t=4$$

```
>> A = [2,1,1,1;1,2,1,1;1,1,2,1;1,1,1,2];B = [1,2,3,4]';
linsolve (A, B)

ans =

-1
0
1
2
```

x = lscov(A,B)	*Solves the equation $A * x = B$ in the least squares sense, i.e., x is the n×1 vector that minimizes the sum of squared errors $(b-A*x)'*(b-A*x)$.*
x = lscov(A,B,V)	*Solves $A*x=B$ in the least squares sense with covariance matrix proportional to V, i.e. x minimizes $(b-A*x)'*inv(V)*(b-A*x)$.*

```
>> A = [2,1,1,1;1,2,1,1;1,1,2,1;1,1,1,2];B = [1,2,3,4]';
lscov (A, B)

ans =

-1
0
1
2
```

X = A\B	*Solves the system $A*X=B$.*

```
>> A = [2,1,1,1;1,2,1,1;1,1,2,1;1,1,1,2];B = [1,2,3,4]';
A\B

ans =

-1.0000
-0.0000
1.0000
2.0000
```

X = A/B	*Solves the system $X*A=B$.*

(continued)

roots (A)	*Returns the roots of the polynomial whose coefficients are given by the vector A (from highest to lowest order).*

As example we find the roots of the polynomial $x^4 + 2x^3 + 3x + 4$

```
>> roots([1 2 3 4])

ans =

-1.6506
-0.1747 + 1. 5469i
-0.1747 - 1. 5469i
```

poly (V)	*Returns the coefficients of the polynomial whose roots are given by the vector V.*

```
>> poly([1 2 3 4])

ans =

1 1 -10 -10 35 -50 24
```

x = fzero x0 (function)	*Returns a zero of the function near x0.*

```
>> X = fzero ('sin (x) - 1', pi/2)

X =

1.5708
```

[x, fval] = fzero x0 (fun)	*Also returns the objective value of the function at x.*

```
>> [F x] = fzero ('sin (x) - 1', pi/2)

X =

1.5708

f =

0
```

The Biconjugate Gradient Method

Below are the MATLAB commands that can be used to solve equations and systems of equations by the biconjugate gradient method.

x = bicg(A,b)

Tries to solve the system Ax = b by the method of biconjugate gradients.

```
>> A = [2 pi * pi 3 * pi - pi; 1 0 - 1 2; exp(1) exp(2) exp(3)
exp(4); i 2i 3i - i];
>> B = [1 2 3 4]';
>> bicg (A, B)
bicg stopped at iteration 4 without converging to the desired
tolerance 1e-006
because the maximum number of iterations was reached. The iterate
returned (number 0) has relative residual 1

ans =

0
0
0
0
```

bicg(A,b,tol)

bicg(A,b,tol,maxit)

Solves Ax = b by specifying tolerance.

Solves Ax = b by specifying the tolerance and the maximum number of iterations.

```
>> bicg(A,B, 1e-009,100)

ans =

1. 0e + 016 *

4.1449 0. 7033i
-7.1997 + 1. 2216i
3.2729 0. 5553i
-0.4360 + 0. 0740i
```

bicg(A,b,tol,maxit,M)

bicg(A,b,tol,maxit,M1,M2)

bicg(A,b,tol,maxit,M1,M2,x0)

[x,f] = bicg(A,b,...)

*Solves the system inv(M) * A * x = inv (M) * b.*

*Solves the system inv(M) * A * x = inv (M) * b with M = M1 * M2.*

*Solves the system inv(M) * A * x = inv (M) * b with M = M1 * M2 and initial value x0.*

Tries to solve the system and also returns a convergence indicator f (0 = convergence, 1 = no-convergence, 2 = ill-conditioned, 3 = stagnation and 4 = very extreme numbers).

```
>> [x, f] = bicg(A,B, 1e-009,100)
x =

1. 0e + 016 *

4.1449 0. 7033i
-7.1997 + 1. 2216i
3.2729 0. 5553i
-0.4360 + 0. 0740i

f =

3
```

(continued)

x = bicgstab(A,b)	*Tries to solve the system Ax = b by the method of stabilized biconjugate gradients.*

```
>> bicgstab (A, B)
bicgstab stopped at iteration 4 without converging to the desired
tolerance 1e-006
because the maximum number of iterations was reached.
The iterate returned (number 4) has relative residual 0.88

ans =

1. 0e + 011 *

0.6696-0. 4857i
-1.1631 + 0. 8437i
0.5287 0. 3835i
-0.0704 + 0. 0511i
```

bicgstab(A,b,tol)	*Solves Ax = b by specifying tolerance.*
bicgstab(A,b,tol,maxit)	*Solves Ax = b by specifying the tolerance and the maximum number of iterations.*

```
>> bicg(A,B, 1e-009,100)

ans =

1. 0e + 016 *

4.1449 0. 7033i
-7.1997 + 1. 2216i
3.2729 0. 5553i
-0.4360 + 0. 0740i
```

(continued)

bicgstab(A,b,tol,maxit,M)	*Solves the system inv(M) * A * x = inv (M) * b.*
bicgstab(A,b,tol,maxit,M1,M2)	*Solves the system inv(M) * A * x = inv (M) * b with M = M1 * M2.*
bicgstab(A,b,tol,maxit, M1,M2,x0)	*Solves the system inv(M) * A * x = inv (M) * b with M = M1 * M2 and initial value x0.*
[x,f] = bicgstab(A,b,...) **[x,f,relres] = bicgstab(A,b,...)**	*Tries to solve the system and returns a convergence indicator f (0 = convergence, 1 = no-convergence, 2 =ill-conditioned, 3 = stagnation and 4 = very extreme numbers).*
[x,f,relres,iter] = bicgstab(A,b,...)	*Also returns the relative residual norm(b-A*x) /norm (b)* *Also returns the number of iterations*

```
>> [x, f, r, i] = bicg(A,B, 1e-006,100)

x =

1. 0e + 016 *

4.1449 0. 7033i
-7.1997 + 1. 2216i
3.2729 0. 5553i
-0.4360 + 0. 0740i

f =

3

r =

26.0415

i =

18
```

The Conjugate Gradients Method

Below are the MATLAB commands that are used to solve equations and systems of equations by the method of conjugate gradients.

x = pcg(A,b)	*Tries to solve the system Ax = b by the pre-conditioned conjugate gradients method.*
pcg(A,b,tol)	*Solves Ax = b by specifying tolerance.*
pcg(A,b,tol,maxit)	*Solves Ax = b by specifying the tolerance and the maximum number of iterations.*
pcg(A,b,tol,maxit,M)	*Solves the system inv(M) * A * x = inv (M) * b.*
pcg(A,b,tol,maxit,M1,M2)	*Solves the system inv(M) * A * x = inv (M) * b with M = M1 * M2.*
pcg(A,b,tol,maxit,M1,M2,x0)	*Solves the system inv(M) * A * x = inv (M) * b with M = M1 * M2 and initial value x0.*
[x,f] = pcg(A,b,...)	*Tries to solve the system and returns a convergence indicator f (0 = convergence, 1 = no-convergence, 2 = ill-conditioned, 3 = stagnation and 4 = very extreme numbers).*
[x,f,relres] = pcg(A,b,...)	*Also returns the relative residual norm (b-A*x) /norm (b).*
[x,f,relres,iter] = pcg(A,b,...)	*Also returns the number of iterations.*

```
>> A=[pi 2*pi 3*pi -pi; 1 0 -1 2; exp(1) exp(2) exp(3) exp(4);
i 2i 3i -i];
>> B=[1 2 3 4]';
>> [x,f,r,i]=pcg(A,B, 1e-006,1000)

x =

0
0
0
0

f =

4

r =

1

i =

0
```

(continued)

x = lsqr(A,b)	*Tries to solve the system Ax = b by the LSQR method.*
lsqr(A,b,tol)	*Solves Ax = b by specifying tolerance.*
lsqr(A,b,tol,maxit)	*Solves Ax = b by specifying the tolerance and the maximum number of iterations.*
lsqr(A,b,tol,maxit,M)	*Solves the system inv(M) * A * x = inv (M) * b.*
lsqr(A,b,tol,maxit,M1,M2)	*Solves the system inv(M) * A * x = inv (M) * b with M = M1 * M2.*
lsqr(A,b,tol,maxit,M1,M2,x0)	*Solves the system inv(M) * A * x = inv (M) * b with M = M1 * M2 and initial value x0.*
[x,f] = lsqr(A,b,...)	*Tries to solve the system and returns a convergence indicator f (0 = convergence, 1 = no-convergence, 2 = ill-conditioned, 3 = stagnation and 4 = very extreme numbers).*
[x,f,relres] = lsqr(A,b,...)	*Also returns the relative residual norm (b-A*x) /norm (b).*
[x,f,relres,iter] = lsqr(A,b,...)	*Also returns the number of iterations.*

```
>> A=[pi 2*pi 3*pi -pi; 1 0 -1 2; exp(1) exp(2) exp(3) exp(4);
i 2i 3i -i];
>> B = [1 2 3 4]';
>> [x, f, r, i] = lsqr(A,B, 1e-006,1000)

x =

1.1869 0. 0910i
0.4295 0. 0705i
-0.5402 - 0. 0362i
0.1364 + 0. 0274i

f =

0

r =

0.6981

i =

3
```

The Residual Method

Below are the MATLAB commands that are used to solve equations and systems of equations by the residual method.

x = qmr(A,b)	*Tries to solve the system Ax = b by the quasi-minimal residual method.*
qmr(A,b,tol)	*Solves Ax = b by specifying tolerance.*
qmr(A,b,tol,maxit)	*Solves Ax = b by specifying the tolerance and the maximum number of iterations.*
qmr(A,b,tol,maxit,M)	*Solves the system inv(M) * A * x = inv (M) * b.*
qmr(A,b,tol,maxit,M1,M2)	*Solves the system inv(M) * A * x = inv (M) * b with M = M1 * M2.*
qmr(A,b,tol,maxit,M1,M2,x0)	*Solves the system inv(M) * A * x = inv (M) * b with M = M1 * M2 and initial value x0.*
[x,f] = qmr(A,b,...)	*Tries to solve the system and returns a convergence indicator f (0 = convergence, 1 = no-convergence, 2 = ill-conditioned, 3 = stagnation and 4 = very extreme numbers).*
[x,f,relres] = qmr(A,b,...)	*Also returns the residual norm (b-A*x) /norm (b).*
[x,f,relres,iter] = qmr(A,b,...)	*Also returns the number of iterations.*

```
>> A=[pi 2*pi 3*pi -pi; 1 0 -1 2; exp(1) exp(2) exp(3) exp(4);
i 2i 3i -i];
>> B=[1 2 3 4]';
>> [x,f,r,i]=qmr(A,B, 1e-006,1000)

x =

1.0e+016 *

0.4810 - 4.0071i
-0.8356 + 6.9603i
0.3798 - 3.1640i
-0.0506 + 0.4215i

f =

3

r =

19.5999

i =

11
```

(continued)

x = gmres(A,b)	*Tries to solve the system Ax = b by the generalized minimum residual method.*
gmres(A,b,tol)	*Solves Ax = b by specifying tolerance.*
gmres(A,b,tol,maxit)	*Solves Ax = b by specifying the tolerance and the maximum number of iterations.*
gmres(A,b,tol,maxit,M)	*Solves the system inv(M) * A * x = inv (M) * b.*
gmres(A,b,tol,maxit,M1,M2)	*Solves the system inv(M) * A * x = inv (M) * b with M = M1 * M2.*
gmres(A,b,tol,maxit,M1,M2,x0)	*Solves the system inv(M) * A * x = inv (M) * b with M = M1 * M2 and initial value x0.*
[x,f] = gmres(A,b,...)	*Tries to solve the system and returns a convergence indicator f (0 = convergence, 1 = no-convergence, 2 = ill-convergence, 3 = stagnation and 4 = very extreme numbers).*
[x,f,relres] = gmres(A,b,...)	*Also returns the relative residual norm(b-A*x) /norm (b).*
[x,f,relres,iter] = gmres(A,b,...)	*Also returns the number of iterations.*

```
>> A=[pi 2*pi 3*pi -pi; 1 0 -1 2; exp(1) exp(2) exp(3) exp(4);
i 2i 3i -i];
>> B=[1 2 3 4]';

>> [x,f,r,i]=gmres(A,B)
x =

1.5504 + 0.0085i
-0.2019 - 0.2433i
-0.2532 + 0.0423i
0.0982 + 0.0169i


f =

3

r =

0.6981

i =

1       4
```

(continued)

x = minres(A,b)	*Tries to solve the system Ax = b by the minimum residual method.*
minres(A,b,tol)	*Solves Ax = b by specifying tolerance.*
minres(A,b,tol,maxit)	*Solves Ax = b by specifying the tolerance and the maximum number of iterations.*
minres(A,b,tol,maxit,M)	*Solves the system inv(M) * A * x = inv (M) * b.*
minres(A,b,tol,maxit,M1,M2)	*Solves the system inv(M) * A * x = inv (M) * b with M = M1 * M2.*
minres(A,b,tol,maxit,M1,M2,x0)	*Solves the system inv(M) * A * x = inv (M) * b with M = M1 * M2 and initial value x0.*
[x,f] = minres(A,b,...)	*Tries to solve the system and returns a convergence indicator f (0 = convergence, 1 = no-convergence, 2 =ill-conditioned, 3 = stagnation and 4 = very extreme numbers).*
[x,f,relres] = minres(A,b,...)	*Also returns the relative residual norm (b-A*x) /norm (b).*
[x,f,relres,iter] = minres(A,b,...)	*Also returns the number of iterations.*

```
>> A=[pi 2*pi 3*pi -pi; 1 0 -1 2; exp(1) exp(2) exp(3) exp(4);
i 2i 3i -i];
>> B=[1 2 3 4]';

>> [x,f,r,i]=minres(A,B, 1e-006,1000)

x =

0.0748 - 0.0070i
-0.0761 - 0.0001i
0.5934 - 0.1085i
-0.1528 + 0.0380i

f =

1

r =

0.0592

i =

1000
```

The Symmetric and Non-negative Least Squares Methods

Below are the MATLAB commands that are used to solve equations and systems of equations by the symmetric and non-negative least squares methods.

x = symmlq(A,b)	*Tries to solve the system Ax = b by the symmetric LQ method.*
symmlq(A,b,tol)	*Solves Ax = b by specifying the tolerance.*
symmlq(A,b,tol,maxit)	*Solves Ax = b by specifying the tolerance and the maximum number of iterations.*
symmlq(A,b,tol,maxit,M)	*Solves the system inv(M) * A * x = inv (M) * b.*
symmlq(A,b,tol,maxit,M1,M2)	*Solves the system inv(M) * A * x = inv (M) * b with M = M1 * M2.*
symmlq(A,b,tol,maxit,M1,M2,x0)	*Solves the system inv(M) * A * x = inv (M) * b with M = M1 * M2 and initial value x0.*
[x,flag] = symmlq(A,b,...)	*Tries to solve the system and returns a convergence indicator (0 = convergence, 1 = no-convergence, 2 = ill-conditioned, 3 = stagnation and 4 = very extreme numbers).*
[x,flag,relres] = symmlq(A,b,...)	*Also returns the relative residual norm (b-A*x) /norm (b).*
[x,flag,relres,iter] = symmlq(A,b,...)	*Also returns the number of iterations.*

```
>> A=[pi 2*pi 3*pi -pi; 1 0 -1 2; exp(1) exp(2) exp(3) exp(4);
i 2i 3i -i];
>> B=[1 2 3 4]';

>> [x,f,r,i]=symmlq(A,B, 1e-006,1000)

x =

0.0121 - 0.0004i
0.0035 - 0.0001i
0.1467 - 0.0061i
0.0001 + 0.0039i

f =

1

r =

0.8325

i =

3
```

(continued)

x = lsqnonneg(C,d)	*Returns the vector x that minimizes norm(C*x-d) subject to x >=0. C and d must be real.*
x = lsqnonneg(C,d,x0) **x = lsqnonneg(C,d,x0,opt)**	*Uses x0 ≥ 0 as the initial value and a possible option. The options are TolX for termination tolerance on x and Display to show the output ('off' does not display output, 'final' shows just the final output and 'notify' shows the output only if there is no convergence).*
[x,resnorm] = lsqnonneg(...)	*Returns the value of the squared 2-norm of the residual: norm(C*x-d)^2.*
[x,resnorm,residual] = lsqnonneg(...)	*In addition returns the residual C * x-d.*
[x,resnorm,residual,f] = lsqnonneg(...)	*In addition gives a convergence indicator f (positive indicates convergence, 0 indicates non-convergence).*
[x,resnorm,residual,f,out,lambda] = lsqnonneg(...)	*In addition to the above, returns output data describing the algorithm used, iterations taken and exit message, and also the vector of Lagrange multipliers lambda.*

```
>> A=[1 2 3;5 7 1;2 3 6]; B=[1 3 5]'; lsqnonneg(A,B)

ans =

0.4857
0
0.5714
```

Solving Linear Systems of Equations

In the previous sections we have studied equations and systems in general. We will now focus on linear systems of equations. To solve such systems we could simply use the commands we have seen so far, however MATLAB has a selection of special commands designed especially for linear systems. The following table lists these commands.

X = linsolve (A, B)	*Solves the linear system A * X = B.*
	
	 We solve the system:
	
	 $2x + y + z + t = 1$
	 $x + y + z + t = 2$
	 $x + y + z + 2t = 3$
	 $x + y + z + 2t = 4$
	
	 ```>> A = [2,1,1,1;1,2,1,1;1,1,2,1;1,1,1,2];B = [1,2,3,4]';```
	 ```linsolve (A, B)```
	
	 ```ans =```
	
	 ```-1```
	 ```0```
	 ```1```
	 ```2```

(continued)

[X, R] = linsolve (A, B)	*Solves the linear system $A*X = B$ and additionally returns the reciprocal of the condition number of A if A is square, or the rank of A if A is not square.*

```
>> A = [2,1,1,1;1,2,1,1;1,1,2,1;1,1,1,2];B = [1,2,3,4]';
[X, R] = linsolve (A, B)

X =

-1
0
1
2

R =

0.1429
```

X = linsolve (A, B, options)	*Solve the linear system $A*X = B$ using various options for the matrix A (UT for upper triangular, LT for lower triangular, SYM for symmetric real or complex hermitian, RECT for general rectangular, POSDEF for positive definite, UHESS for upper Hessenberg and TRANSA for conjugate transpose).*
rank (A)	*Rank of the matrix A.*

```
>> rank (A)

ans =

4
```

det (A)	*Determinant of the square matrix A.*

```
>> det (A)

ans =

5
```

Z = null (A, 'r')	*Rational basis for the null space of A.*

Systems of linear equations can be converted to array form and solved using calculations with matrices. A system can be written in the form $M.X = B$, where X is the vector of variables, B the vector of independent terms and M the matrix of coefficients of the system. If M is a square matrix and the determinant of the matrix M is non-null, M is invertible, and the unique solution of the system can be written in the form: $X = M^{-1}B$. In this case, the commands *solve, linsolve, lscov, bicg, pcg, lsqr, gmr, gmres, minres, symmlq* or $M\backslash B$, already described above, offer the solution.

If the determinant of M is zero, the system has infinitely many solutions, since there are rows or columns in M that are linearly dependent. In this case, the number of redundant equations can be calculated to find out how many variables are needed to describe the solutions. If the matrix M is rectangular (not square), the system may be undetermined (the number of equations is less than the number of variables), overdetermined (the number of equations is greater than the number of variables) or non-singular (the number of equations is equal to number of variables and M has non-zero determinant). An indeterminate system can have infinitely many solutions, or none, and likewise for an overdetermined system. If a system has no solution, it is called inconsistent (incompatible), and if there is at least one solution, it is called consistent (compatible). The system $M.X = B$ is called *homogeneous* when the vector B is the null vector, i.e. the system is of the form $M.X = 0$. If the determinant of M is non-null, the unique solution of the system is the null vector (obtained with the command *linsolve*). If the determinant of M is zero, the system has infinitely many solutions. The solutions can be found using the commands *solve*, *linsolve*, *lsqr* or other commands described above for general linear systems.

A fundamental tool in the analysis and solution of systems of equations is the *Rouche-Frobenius theorem*. This theorem says that a system of m equations with n unknowns has a solution if, and only if, the rank of the matrix of coefficients coincides with the rank of the array extended with the vector column of the system-independent terms. If the two ranks are equal, and equal to the number of unknowns, the system has a unique solution. If the two ranks are the same, but less that the number of unknowns, the system has infinitely many solutions. If they are different, the system has no solution.

In summary: Let A be the matrix of coefficients of the system and B the matrix A augmented by the column vector of independent terms.

```
If rank(A) = rank(B), the system is incompatible (without solution).
If rank (A) = rank(B) < n, the system is indefinite (has infinitely many solutions).
If = rank(A) = rank(B) = n, the system has a unique solution.
```

This theorem allows us to analyze the solutions of a system of equations before solving it.

We have already encountered *homogeneous systems*. A system $A.X = B$ is said homogeneous if the vector of independent terms B is null, so every homogeneous system is of the form $A.X = 0$. In a homogeneous system, the rank of the matrix of coefficients and the rank of the matrix augmented to include the column vector of independent terms always coincide. If we apply the Rouche-Frobenius theorem, a homogeneous system will have a unique solution when the determinant of the matrix A is non-zero. Since the null vector is always a solution of a homogeneous system, this must be the unique solution. A homogeneous system will have infinitely many solutions when the determinant of the matrix A is zero. In this case, the solutions are calculated as for general systems (using the command *solve*), or by using the function *null (A)*.

As a first example we solve the system:

$$2x + y + z + t = 1$$
$$x + 2y + z + t = 1$$
$$x + y + 2z + 2t = 1$$
$$x + y + z + 2t = 1$$

We will find the rank of the matrix of the system and the rank of the augmented matrix obtained by extending the matrix by the column vector of independent terms.

```
>> A = [2,1,1,1;1,2,1,1;1,1,2,1;1,1,1,2];
>> B = [2,1,1,1,1;1,2,1,1,1;1,1,2,1,1;1,1,1,2,1];
>> [rank (A), rank (B)]

ans =

4 4
```

We note that the ranks of the two matrices coincide with the number of unknowns. The Rouche-Frobenius theorem then tells us that the system is compatible with a unique solution. We can calculate the solution in the following way:

```
>> B = [1 1 1 1]';
>> linsolve (A, B)

ans =

0.2000
0.2000
0.2000
0.2000
```

The solution could also have been found using the following commands:

```
>> lscov (A, B)

ans =

0.2000
0.2000
0.2000
0.2000

>> bicg (A, B)

bicg converged at iteration 1 to a solution with relative residual 0

ans =

0.2000
0.2000
0.2000
0.2000

>> pcg (A, B)

PCG converged at iteration 1 to a solution with relative residual 0

ans =

0.2000
0.2000
0.2000
0.2000
```

```
>> lsqr (A, B)

lsqr converged at iteration 1 to a solution with relative residual 0

ans =

0.2000
0.2000
0.2000
0.2000

>> qmr (A, B)

QMR converged at iteration 1 to a solution with relative residual 0

ans =

0.2000
0.2000
0.2000
0.2000

>> gmres (A, B)

gmres converged at iteration 1 to a solution with relative residual 1.5e-016

ans =

0.2000
0.2000
0.2000
0.2000

>> symmlq (A, B)

symmlq converged at iteration 1 to a solution with relative residual 0

ans =

0.2000
0.2000
0.2000
0.2000
```

As a second example, we solve the system:

$$x + 2y + 3z = 6$$
$$x + 3y + 8z = 19$$
$$2x + 3y + z = -1$$
$$5x + 6y + 4z = 5$$

We find the rank of the matrix of the system and the rank of the augmented matrix.

```
>> A=[1,2,3;1,3,8;2,3,1;5,6,4];
>> B=[1,2,3,6;1,3,8,19;2,3,1,-1;5,6,4,5];
>> [rank(A), rank(B)]

ans =

3      3
```

We note that the ranks of the two matrices coincide with the number of unknowns. The Rouche-Frobenius theorem then tells us that the system is compatible with a unique solution. We can calculate the solution in the following way:

```
>> A = [1,2,3;1,3,8;2,3,1;5,6,4];
>> B = [19-6 - 5-1]';
>> linsolve (A, B)

ans =

1.0000
-2.0000
3.0000
```

As a third example, we solve the system:

$$x+2y+z=0$$
$$2x-y+z=0$$
$$2x+y\quad=-1$$

As we have a homogeneous system, we will calculate the determinant of the matrix of coefficients of the system.

```
>> A = [1,2, - 1; 2, - 1, 1; 3,1,0];
>> det (A)

ans =

5. 5511e-016
```

This answer is very close to zero, in fact the determinant is actually zero, thus the homogeneous system will have infinitely many solutions, which are calculated with the command *solve* as shown below.

```
>> [x, y, z] = solve('x+2*y-z, 2*x-y+z, 3*x+y', 'x,y,z')

x =

-z1/5

y =

(3 * z1) / 5

z =

z1
```

Thus the infinite set of solutions depend on a parameter z1 and are described as $\{(-z1/5, 3z1/5)\}, \cdots z1 \in R$.

EXERCISE 4-1

Expand the following algebraic expressions:

$$(x+1)(x+2), \frac{x+1}{x+2},$$

$$\sin(x+y), \ \cos(2x), \ e^{a+\ln(b)}, \ln\left(\frac{x}{(1-x)^2}\right), (x+1)(y+z).$$

```
>> syms x y z b t
>> pretty (expand ((x + 1) * (2.4.x+2)))

 2
x + 3 x + 2

>> pretty (expand ((x + 1) / (2.4.x+2)))

  x         1
------ + -------
x + 2     x + 2

>> pretty (expand (sin(x + y)))

sin(x) cos (y) + cos (x) sin(y)
             .
>> pretty (expand (cos(2*x)))

     2
2 cos (x) - 1

>> pretty (expand (exp (a+log (b)))

exp (a) b

>> pretty (expand (log (x/(1-x)^ 2)))

log (x) - 2-log(1-x)

>> pretty (expand ((x + 1) * (y+z)))

x y + x z + y + z
```

EXERCISE 4-2

Factorize the following algebraic expressions:

$$6x^2 + 18x - 24, \quad x^4 - y^4, \quad x^3 + y^3, \quad \frac{x^3 - y^3}{x^4 - y^4}$$

```
>> syms x y
>> pretty (factor(6*x^2+18*x-24))

6 (x + 4) (x - 1)

>> pretty (factor(x^4-y^4))

          2   2
(x y) (x + y) (x + y)

>> pretty (factor(x^3+y^3))

        2         2
(x + y) (x - x y + y )

>> pretty (factor ((x^3-y^3) /(x^4-y^4)))

  2       2
 x + x y + y
-----------------
        2   2
(x + y) (x + y )
```

EXERCISE 4-3

Simplify the following algebraic expressions:

$$\sin^2(x) + \cos^2(x), e^{a+\ln(be^c)}, \cos(3a\cos(x)), \frac{x^2 - y^2}{(x-y)^3}.$$

```
>> syms x y b c
>> simplify (sin (x) ^ 2 + cos (x) ^ 2)

ans =

1
```

```
>> pretty (simplify (exp (a+log (b * exp (c)))))
```

```
b exp(a + c)
```

```
>> pretty (sym (simple (cos (3 * acos (x)))))
```

```
     3
4 x - 3 x
```

```
>> pretty(simple((x^2-y^2) /(x-y) ^ 3))
```

```
x + y
-------
       2
(x - y)
```

EXERCISE 4-4

Rewrite the following algebraic expressions in terms of powers of x:

$$f(x)=a^3x-x+a^3x+a,\cdots p(x)=\frac{y}{x}+\frac{2z}{x}+x^{\frac{1}{3}}-y*x^{\frac{1}{3}},\cdots q(x)=(x+1)(x+2)$$

Rewrite the following expression in terms of powers of $\sin(x)$: $y(\sin(x)+1)+\sin(x)$

Rewrite the following expression in terms of powers of $\ln(x)$: $\cdots f=a\ln(x)-x\ln(x)-x$

Rewrite the following expression in terms of powers of x and y: $p=xy+zxy+yx^2+zxy^2+x+zx$

```
>> syms x y z
>> pretty (collect(a^3*x-x+a^3+a, x))
```

```
   3          3
(a -1) x + a + a
```

```
>> pretty (collect (y / x+2 * z/x + x ^(1/3) - y * ^(1/3) x, x))
```

```
y + 2 z - x 4/3 y + x4/3
----------------------
          x
```

```
>> pretty(collect((x+1) * (x+2)))
```

```
 2
x + 3 x + 2
```

```
>> p = x * y + z * x * y + y * x ^ 2-z * y * x ^ 2 + x + z * x;
>> pretty(collect(p, [x,y]))

      2
(1-z) x y + (z + 1) x y + (z + 1) x

>> f = a * log (x) - log (x) * x-x;

>> pretty (collect (f, log (x)))

(a - x) log (x) - x
```

EXERCISE 4-5

Combine the terms as much as possible in the following expression:

$$a\ln(x)+3\ln(x)-\ln(1-x)+\ln(1+x)/2$$

Simplify it assuming that a is real and x > 0.

```
>> pretty (sym (simple (a * log (x) + 3 * log (x) - log(1-x) + log(1+x)/2)))

log(x + 1)/2- log(1-x) + 3 log (x) + log (x)

>> x = sym ('x', 'positive')

x =

x

>> a = sym ('a', 'real')

a =

a

>> pretty (sym (simple (a * log (x) + 3 * log (x) - log(1-x) + log(1+x)/2)))

      /       x - 1        \
 -log|  -  ---------------- |
      |    3  a       1/2   |
      \   x  x  (x + 1)     /
```

EXERCISE 4-6

Expand and simplify the following trigonometric expressions:

$$(a)\sin[3x]\cos[5x]$$
$$(b)\left[\left(\cot[a]\right)^2\right]+\left(\sec[a]\right)^2-\left(\csc[a]\right)^2$$
$$(c)\sin[a]/\left(1+\cot[a]^2\right)-\sin[a]^3$$

```
>> pretty (simple (expand (sym (sin(3*x) * cos(5*x)))))

sin(8 x)   sin (2 x)
-------- - ---------
   2          2

>> pretty (simple (expand (((cot (a)) ^ 2 + (sec (a)) ^ 2-(csc (a)) ^ 2))))

   1
------- - 1
   2
cos (a)

>> pretty (simple (expand (sin (a) / (1 + cot (a) ^ 2)- sin (a) ^ 3)))

0
```

EXERCISE 4-7

Simplify the following algebraic expressions as much as possible:

```
                             2      2    3   3
  x       y     2 x y    1 + a    1 - b   a - b
-----  - ----- + -----  , -----  + ----- - -----
x + y   x - y    2   2      b        a      a b
                x - y
```

```
>> pretty (simple (expand (x / (x + y) - y /(x-y) + 2 * x * y /(x^2-y^2))))

1

>> pretty (simple (expand ((1+a^2)/b + (1-b ^ 2) /a - (a ^ 3-b ^ 3) /(a*b))))

1   1
- + -
a   b
```

EXERCISE 4-8

Simplify the following algebraic fractions as much as possible:

$$\frac{a^3 - a^2b + ac^2 - bc^2}{a^3 + ac^2 + a^2b + b c^2}, \quad \frac{(x^2 - 9)(x^2 - 2x + 1)(x - 3)}{(x^2 - 6x + 9)(x^2 - 1)(x - 1)}$$

```
>> pretty(simple(factor(a^3-a^2*b+a*c^2-b*c^2)/(a^3+a*c^2+a^2*b+b*c^2)))
```

```
a - b
-----
a + b
```

```
>> pretty(simple(factor((x^2-9)*(x^2-2*x+1)*(x-3))/((x^2-6*x+9)*(x^2-1) *(x-1))))
```

```
  2
----- + 1
x + 1
```

EXERCISE 4-9

Calculate the roots of the following polynomials:

$$x^3 - 6x^2 - 72x - 27, \quad 2x^4 - 3x^3 + 4x^2 - 5x + 11, \quad x^{11} - 1$$

Evaluate the first polynomial at the identity matrix of order 3, the second at the unit matrix of order 3 and the third at a uniformly random matrix of order 3.

Find the coefficients of the derivatives of the given polynomials and display the results in polynomial form.

```
>> p1 = [1 - 6 -72 - 27]; r = roots (p)
```

```
r =

12.1229
-5.7345
-0.3884
```

```
>> p2 = [2 -3 4 -5 11];r=roots(p)
```

```
r =

1.2817 + 1.0040i
1.2817 - 1.0040i
-0.5317 + 1.3387i
-0.5317 - 1.3387i
```

```
>> p3 = [1 0 0 0 0 0 0 0 0 0 0 1]; r = roots (p)

r =

-1.0000
-0.8413 + 0. 5406i
-0.8413 - 0. 5406i
-0.4154 + 0. 9096i
-0.4154 - 0. 9096i
0.1423 + 0. 9898i
0.1423 0. 9898i
0.6549 + 0. 7557i
0.6549-0. 7557i
0.9595 + 0. 2817i
0.9595 0. 2817i

>> Y1 = polyval (p1, eye (3))

Y1 =

-104 - 27 - 27
-27  -104 - 27
-27   - 27 -104

>> Y2 = polyval (p2, ones (3))

Y2 =

9 -9 -9
9 -9 -9
9 -9 -9

>> Y3 = polyval (p3, rand (3))

Y3 =

1.1050 1.3691 1.0000
1.3368 1.0065 1.0013
1.0000 1.0000 1.6202

>> d1 = polyder (p1)

D1 =

3 -12 -72

>> pretty (poly2sym(d1,'x'))

    2
3 x - 12 x - 72
```

```
>> d2 = polyder (p2)

D2 =

8 -9  8 - 5

>> pretty (poly2sym(d2,'x'))

   3     2
8 x - 9 x + 8 x - 5

>> d3 = polyder (p3)

D3 =

11    0    0    0    0    0    0    0    0    0    0

>> pretty (poly2sym(d3,'x'))

     10
11 x
```

EXERCISE 4-10

Consider the equally spaced set of points in the interval [0,5] separated by one tenth. Interpolate the error function at these points and adjust a polynomial of degree 6 thereto. Represent the original curve and the interpolated on the same graph.

```
>> x = (0: 0.1: 5)';
y = erf (x);
f = polyval(p,x);
>> p = polyfit(x,y,6)

p =

0.0012 - 0.0173 0.0812 - 0.0791 - 0.4495 1.3107 - 0.0128

>> f = polyval(p,x);
plot(x,y,'o',x,f,'-')
axis([0 5 0 2])
```

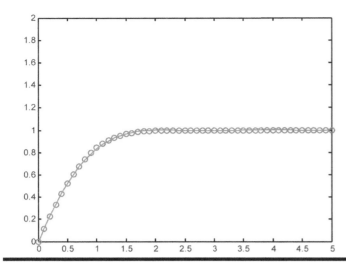

EXERCISE 4-11

Calculate the second degree interpolating polynomial passing through the points (- 1,4), (0,2), and (1,6) in the least squares sense.

```
>> x = [- 1, 0, 1];y=[4,2,6];p=poly2sym(polyfit(x,y,2))

p =

3 * x ^ 2 + x + 2
```

EXERCISE 4-12

Represent 200 points of cubic interpolation between the points (x, y) given by y= e^x for x values in 20 equally spaced intervals between 0 and 2.

First, we define the 20 points *(x, y)*, for *x* equally spaced between 0 and 2:

```
>> x = 0:0.1:2;
>> y = exp(x);
```

Now we find cubic interpolation points *(xi, yi)*, for *x* values in 200 equally spaced between 0 and 2, and represent them on a graph together with the initial points *(x, y)* (indicated by asterisks).

```
>> xi = 0:0. 01:2;
>> yi = interp1(x,y,xi,'cubic');
>> plot(x,y,'*',xi,yi)
```

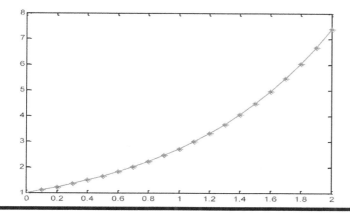

EXERCISE 4-13

Find interpolation points of the parametric function X = cosh (t), Y = sinh (t), Z = tanh (t) for values of t between 0 and π /6 in 25 equally spaced intervals.

First, we define the given points (x, y, z), for equally spaced values of t between 0 and π /6.

```
>> t = 0: pi/150: pi/6;
>> x = cosh (t); y = sinh (t); z = tanh (t);
```

Now we find the 26 points of interpolation (x_i, y_i, z_i), for values of the parameter t equally spaced between 0 and π /6.

```
>> xi = cosh (t); yi = sinh (t);
>> zi = griddata(x,y,z,xi,yi);
>> points = [xi, yi, zi]

points =

1.0000 0 0
1.0002 0.0209 0.0209
1.0009 0.0419 0.0419
1.0020 0.0629 0.0627
1.0035 0.0839 0.0836
1.0055 0.1049 0.1043
1.0079 0.1260 0.1250
1.0108 0.1471 0.1456
1.0141 0.1683 0.1660
1.0178 0.1896 0.1863
1.0220 0.2110 0.2064
1.0267 0.2324 0.2264
1.0317 0.2540 0.2462
1.0373 0.2756 0.2657
1.0433 0.2974 0.2851
```

```
1.0498 0.3194 0.3042
1.0567 0.3414 0.3231
1.0641 0.3636 0.3417
1.0719 0.3860 0.3601
1.0802 0.4085 0.3782
1.0890 0.4312 0.3960
1.0983 0.4541 0.4135
1.1080 0.4772 0.4307
1.1183 0.5006 0.4476
1.1290 0.5241 0.4642
1.1402 0.5479 0.4805
```

EXERCISE 4-14

Using fast Fourier transform (FFT) interpolation, find the 30 points (xi, yi) approximating the function y = sinh (x) for values of x that are in equally spaced intervals between 0 and 2π, interpolating them between values of (x, y) given by y = sinh (x) for x values in 20 evenly spaced intervals in (0,2π). Graph the points.

First, we define the *x* values equally spaced in 20 intervals between 0 and 2π.

```
>> x =(0:pi/10:2*pi);
```

Now we find the interpolation points *(x, y)*.

```
>> y = interpft (sinh (x), 30);
>> points = [y ', (asinh (y))']
```

```
points =

-0.0000 - 0.0000
-28.2506 - 4.0346
23.3719 3.8451
-4.9711 - 2.3067
-7.7918 - 2.7503
14.0406 3.3364
-4.8129 - 2.2751
-0.8717 - 0.7877
11.5537 3.1420
-3.3804 - 1.9323
4.4531 2.1991
11.8616 3.1682
-0.2121 - 0.2105
10.9811 3.0914
15.1648 3.4132
6.1408 2.5147
21.2540 3.7502
23.3792 3.8455
18.5918 3.6166
39.4061 4.3672
```

```
40.6473 4.3982
42.8049 4.4499
73.2876 4.9876
74.8962 5.0093
89.7159 5.1898
139.0371 5.6279
139.3869 5.6304
180.2289 5.8874
282.4798 6.3368
201.7871 6.0004
```

```
>> plot (points)
```

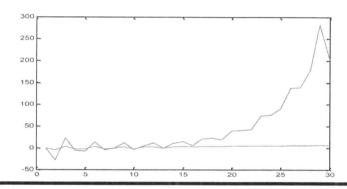

EXERCISE 4-15

Find the polynomial of degree 3 which is the best fit through the points (i, i^2) $1 \le i \le 7$, in the least squares sense. Evaluate this polynomial at $x = 10$ and graphically represent the best fit curve.

```
>> x =(1:7);y=[1,4,9,16,25,36,49];p=vpa(poly2sym(polyfit(x,y,2))))
```

```
p =
```

```
x ^ 2 - 0.000000000000009169181662272871686413366801652 * x +
0.000000000000002076189147201592452636365781895317
```

Now we calculate the numerical value of the polynomial p at $x = 10$.

```
>> subs(p,10)
```

```
ans =
```

```
100.0000
```

Next we graph the polynomial:

```
>> ezplot(p,[-5,5])
```

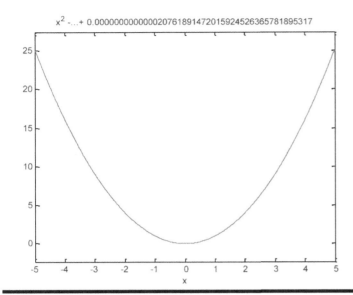

$x^2 - \ldots + 0.00000000000002076189147201592452636578189531 7$

EXERCISE 4-16

Find the solutions to the following equations:

$$\sin(x)\cos(x)=0, \sin(x)=a\cos(x), ax\wedge 2+bx+c=0 \ and \sin(x)+\cos(x)= sqrt(3)/2$$

```
>> solve ('sin (x) * cos (x) = 0')

ans =

[        0]
[1/2 * pi]
[-1/2 * pi]

>> solve ('sin (x) = a * cos (x) ',' x')

ans =

atan (a)

>> solve('a*x^2+b*x+c=0','x')

ans =

[1/2/a * (-b + (b ^ 2-4 * a * c) ^(1/2))]
[1/2/a * (-b-(b^2-4*a*c) ^(1/2))]
```

```
>> solve (' sin (x) + cos (x) = sqrt (3) / 2')

ans =

[1/2 * 3 ^(1/2)]
[1/2 * 3 ^(1/2)]
```

EXERCISE 4-17

Find at least two solutions for each of the following two trigonometric and exponential equations:

$$x\sin(x) = \frac{1}{2} \; and \; 2^{x^3} = 4(2^{3x})$$

First, we use the command *solve*:

```
>> vpa (solve ('x * sin (x) = 1/2 ', 'x'))

ans =

matrix([[-226.19688152398440474751335389781]])

>> vpa (solve ('2 ^(x^3) = 4 * 2 ^(3*x)', 'x'))

ans =

2.0
-1.0
-1.0
```

For the first equation we get no solutions, but for the second we do. To better analyze the first equation, we graphically represent the function to determine approximate intervals where the possible solutions can be found.

```
>> fplot ('[x * sin (x) - 1/2.0]', [0, 4 * pi])
```

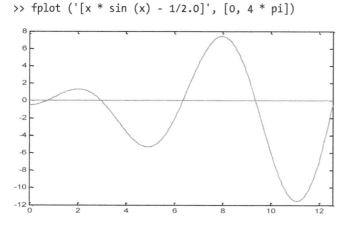

We observe that there is a solution between 0 and 2, another between 2 and 4, another between 4 and 8, and so on. We can calculate three of them with the command *fzero*.

```
>> s1 = fzero ('x * sin (x) - 1/2 ', 2)

s1 =

0.7408

>> s2 = fzero ('x * sin (x) - 1/2 ', 4)

s2 =

2.9726

>> s3 = fzero ('x * sin (x) - 1/2 ', 6)

S3 =

6.3619
```

EXERCISE 4-18

Solve each of the following two logarithmic and surd equations:

$$x^{3/2}\log(x)=x\log(x^{3/2}),\cdots sqrt[1-x]+sqrt[1+x]=a.$$

```
>> vpa (solve ('^(3/2) x * log (x) = x * log (x) ^(3/2)'))

ans =

1.0
0.31813150520476413531265425158766 1.33723570143068940089011621431937 * i
```

We graph the function to determine the intervals in which a solution can be found. The plot indicates that x=1 is the only real solution.

```
>> fplot ('[^(3/2) x * log (x), x * log (x) ^(3/2)]', [0.3, - 1, 6])
```

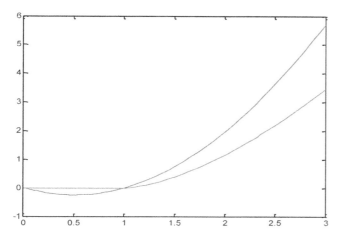

Now, we solve the surd equation:

```
>> pretty (sym (solve ('sqrt(1-x) + sqrt (1 + x) = a ', 'x')))
```

```
+-                 -+
|            2 1/2  |
|    a (4 - a )     |
|    -------------  |
|          2        |
|                   |
|            2 1/2  |
|    a (4 - a )     |
|  - -------------  |
|          2        |
+-                 -+
```

EXERCISE 4-19

Solve the following system of two equations:

$$\cos(x/12)/\exp\left(x^2/16\right)=y$$
$$-5/4+y=\sin\left(x^{3/2}\right)$$

```
>> [x, y] = solve ('cos(x/12) /exp(x^2/16) = y ',' - 5/4 + y = sin (x ^(3/2))')
```

```
x =
```

0.34569744170126319331033283636228 * i - 0.18864189802267887925036526820236

```
y =
```

0.0086520715192230549621145978569268 * i + 1.0055146234480859930589058368368

EXERCISE 4-20

Find the intersection of the hyperbolas with equations $X^2 - Y = r^2$ and $a^2 X^2 - b^2 Y^2 = a^2 b^2$ with the parabola $z^2 = 2px$.

```
>> [x, y, z] = solve('a^2*x^2-b^2*y^2=a^2*b^2','x^2-y^2=r^2','z^2=2*p*x','x,y,z')

x =

((4*a^2*b^2*p^2-4*b^2*p^2*r^2) /(a^2-b^2)) ^(1/2) /(2*p)
((4*a^2*b^2*p^2-4*b^2*p^2*r^2) /(a^2-b^2)) ^(1/2) /(2*p)
((4*a^2*b^2*p^2-4*b^2*p^2*r^2) /(a^2-b^2)) ^(1/2) /(2*p)
-((4*a^2*b^2*p^2-4*b^2*p^2*r^2) /(a^2-b^2)) ^(1/2) /(2*p)
((4*a^2*b^2*p^2-4*b^2*p^2*r^2) /(a^2-b^2)) ^(1/2) /(2*p)
-((4*a^2*b^2*p^2-4*b^2*p^2*r^2) /(a^2-b^2)) ^(1/2) /(2*p)
-((4*a^2*b^2*p^2-4*b^2*p^2*r^2) /(a^2-b^2)) ^(1/2) /(2*p)
-((4*a^2*b^2*p^2-4*b^2*p^2*r^2) /(a^2-b^2)) ^(1/2) /(2*p)


y =

a * ((b^2-r^2) /(a^2-b^2)) ^(1/2)
-a * ((b^2-r^2) /(a^2-b^2)) ^(1/2)
a * ((b^2-r^2) /(a^2-b^2)) ^(1/2)
a * ((b^2-r^2) /(a^2-b^2)) ^(1/2)
-a * ((b^2-r^2) /(a^2-b^2)) ^(1/2)
a * ((b^2-r^2) /(a^2-b^2)) ^(1/2)
-a * ((b^2-r^2) /(a^2-b^2)) ^(1/2)
-a * ((b^2-r^2) /(a^2-b^2)) ^(1/2)


z =

((4*a^2*b^2*p^2-4*b^2*p^2*r^2) /(a^2-b^2)) ^(1/4)
((4*a^2*b^2*p^2-4*b^2*p^2*r^2) /(a^2-b^2)) ^(1/4)
-((4*a^2*b^2*p^2-4*b^2*p^2*r^2) /(a^2-b^2)) ^(1/4)
((4*a^2*b^2*p^2-4*b^2*p^2*r^2) /(a^2-b^2)) ^(1/4) * i
-((4*a^2*b^2*p^2-4*b^2*p^2*r^2) /(a^2-b^2)) ^(1/4)
-((4*a^2*b^2*p^2-4*b^2*p^2*r^2) /(a^2-b^2)) ^(1/4) * i
((4*a^2*b^2*p^2-4*b^2*p^2*r^2) /(a^2-b^2)) ^(1/4) * i
-((4*a^2*b^2*p^2-4*b^2*p^2*r^2) /(a^2-b^2)) ^(1/4) * i
```

EXERCISE 4-21

Study and solve the system:

$$x_1 - x_2 + x_3 \quad = 1$$
$$4x_1 + 5x_2 - 5x_3 = 4$$
$$2x_1 + x_2 - x_3 \quad = 2$$
$$x_1 + 2x_2 - 2x_3 \quad = 1$$

```
>> A = [1, - 1, 1; 4, 5, - 5; 2, 1, - 1; 1, 2, - 2]

A =

1  -1 -1
5  -4 -5
2  -1 -1
2  -1 -2

>> B = [1, - 1, 1, 1; 4, 5, - 5, 4; 2, 1, - 1, 2; 1, 2, - 2, 1]

B =

1 -1 -1 -1
5  4 -5  4
1  2 -1  2
2  1 -2  1

>> [rank (A), rank (B)]

ans =

2 2
```

We see that the ranks of *A* and *B* coincide and its value is 2, which is less than the number of unknowns in the system (3). Therefore, the system will have infinitely many solutions. We try to solve it with the command *solve*:

```
>> [x 1, x 2, x 3] = solve('x1-x2+x3=1','4*x1+5*x2-5*x3=4','2*x1+x2-x3=2',
'x1+2*x2-2*x3=1','x1','x2','x3')
```

Warning: 4 equations in three variables.

```
x 1 =

1

x 2 =

z

x 3 =

z
```

Infinitely many solutions are obtained in terms of the parameter *z*, namely *{1, z, z}*, *z*∈ *R*. Note that the trivial solution {1,0,0} is obtained by setting the parameter equal to zero.

EXERCISE 4-22

Study and solve the system:

$$x+2y+3z+t = 6$$
$$x+3y+8z+t = 19$$

```
>> A = [1,2,3,1;1,3,8,1]

A =

1 2 3 1
1 3 8 1

>> B = [1,2,3,1,6;1,3,8,1,19]

B =

1 2 3 1  6
1 3 8 1 19

>> [rank (A), rank (B)]

ans =

2 2
```

We see that the ranks of A and B coincide, and their common value is 2, which is less than the number of unknowns for the system (4). Therefore, the system has infinitely many solutions. We try to solve it:

```
>> [x, y, z, t] = solve('x+2*y+3*z+t=6','x+3*y+8*z+t=19','x','y','z','t')

Warning: 2 equations in 4 variables. New variables might be introduced.

x =

7 * z1 - z2 - 20

y =

z2

z =

13 - 5 * z1

t =

z1
```

This time the solution depends on two parameters z1 and z2. As these parameters vary over the real numbers (x,y,z,t) varies over all solutions of the system. These solutions form a two-dimensional subspace of the four dimensional real vector space which can be expressed as follows:

$$\{7z1 - z2 - 20, z2, 13 - 5z1, z1\} \cdot \cdot z1, z2 \in R$$

EXERCISE 4-23

Study and solve the system:

$$3x_1 + x_2 + x_3 - x_4 = 0$$
$$2x_1 + x_2 - x_3 + x_4 = 0$$
$$x_1 + 2x_2 + 4x_3 + 2x_4 = 0$$
$$2x_1 + x_2 - 2x_3 - x_4 = 0$$

```
>> det ([3,1,1,-1;2,1,-1,1;1,2,4,2;2,1,-2,-1])

ans =

-30
```

As the determinant of the coefficient matrix is non-zero, the system has only the trivial solution:

```
>> [(x1,x2,x3,x4]=solve('3*x1+x2+x3-x4=0','2*x1+x2-x3+x4=0','x1+2*x2-4*x3-2*x4=0',
'x1-x2-3*x3-5*x4=0','x1','x2','x3','x4')]

x 1 =

0

x 2 =

0

x 3 =

0

x 4 =

0
```

EXERCISE 4-24

Study and solve the following system, according to the values of m:

$$mx + y + z = 1$$
$$x + my + z = m$$
$$x + y + mz = m^2$$

```
>> syms m
>> A=[m,1,1;1,m,1;1,1,m]

A =

[ m, 1, 1]
[ 1, m, 1]
[ 1, 1, m]

>> det(A)

ans =

m^3 - 3*m + 2
```

```
>> solve('m^3 - 3*m + 2=0','m')
```

ans =

-2
1
1

The values of *m* which determine the rank of the matrix are - 2 and 1.

We now consider the augmented matrix extended to include a fourth column with values *1*, *m* and m^2:

```
>> B=[m,1,1,1;1,m,1,m;1,1,m,m^2]
```

B =

```
[ m, 1, 1,    1]
[ 1, m, 1,    m]
[ 1, 1, m, m^2]
```

We will study the case *m =-2*:

```
>> rank(subs(A,{m},{-2}))
```

ans =

2

```
>> rank(subs(B,{m},{-2}))
```

ans =

3

We see that the ranks of the two arrays are different, hence the system is inconsistent (i.e. it has no solution) if *m =-2*.

Now we study the case *m = 1*:

```
>> rank(subs(A,{m},{1}))
```

ans =

1

```
>> rank(subs(B,{m},{1}))
```

ans =

1

Now the rank of both matrices is 1, which is less than the number of unknowns. In this case, the system has infinitely many solutions. We find them by substituting $m = 1$ into the initial system:

```
>> [x,y,z]=solve('x+y+z=1','x','y','z')
Warning: 1 equation in 3 variables. New variables might be introduced.
```

```
x =
```

```
1 - z2 - z1
```

```
y =
```

```
z2
```

```
z =
```

```
z1
```

Thus the solutions are given in terms of two parameters. The two-dimensional subspace of solutions is:

$$\{1-z2-z1,z2,z1\},\cdots z1,z2 \in R$$

If we consider the case where m is neither - 2 nor 1, the system has a unique solution, which is given by the command *solve*:

```
>> [x,y,z]=solve('m*x+y+z=1','x+m*y+z=m','x+y+m*z=m^2','x','y','z')
```

```
x =
```

```
-(m + 1)/(m + 2)
```

```
y =
```

```
1 /(m + 2)
```

```
z =
```

```
(m ^ 2 + 2 * m + 1) /(m + 2)
```

EXERCISE 4-25

Study and solve the following system, according to the values of m:

$$my = m$$
$$(1+m)x - z = m$$
$$y + z = m$$

```
>> syms m
>> A = [0, m, 0; m + 1, 0, - 1; 0,1,1]

A =

[    0, m,   0]
[m + 1, 0, - 1]
[    0, 1,   1]

>> det (A)

ans =

-m ^ 2 - m

>> solve('-m^2-m=0','m')

ans =

-1
0
```

We see that the values of *m* which determine the rank of the matrix of coefficients of the system are *m = 1* and *m = 0.*

We now consider the augmented matrix:

```
>> B = [0, m, 0, m; m + 1, 0, - 1, m; 0,1,1,m]

B =

[0, m, 0, m]
[m + 1, 0, - 1, m]
[0, 1, 1, m]
```

```
>> rank (subs(A,{m},{-1}))

ans =

2

>> rank (subs(B,{m},{-1}))

ans =

3
```

If $m = -1$, we see that the system has no solution because the rank of the matrix of coefficients of the system is 2 and the rank of the augmented matrix is 3.

Now, we analyze the case $m = 0$:

When m is zero the system is homogeneous, since the independent terms are all null. We analyze the determinant of the matrix of coefficients of the system.

```
>> det (subs(A,{m},{0}))

ans =

0
```

Since the determinant is zero, the system has infinitely many solutions:

```
>> [x, y, z] = solve('x-z=0','y+z=0','x','y','z')
Warning: 2 equations in three variables. New variables might be introduced.

x =

z1

y =

-z1

z =

z1
```

Thus the solutions are given in terms of one parameter. The one-dimensional subspace of solutions is:

$$\{z1, -z1, z1\} \cdots z1 \in R$$

If m is neither 0 nor - 1, the system has a unique solution, since the ranks of the matrix of the system and of the augmented matrix coincide. The solution, using the function *solve*, is calculated as follows.

```
>> [x, y, z] = solve ('m * y = m', '(1+m) * x-z = m ',' y + z = m', 'x', 'y', 'z')

x =

(2 * m - 1) /(m + 1)

y =

1

z =

m - 1
```

EXERCISE 4-26

Study and solve the system:

$$2x + y + z + t = 1$$
$$x + 2y + z + t = 1$$
$$x + y + 2z + t = 1$$
$$x + y + z + 2t = 1$$

```
>> A=[2,1,1,1;1,2,1,1;1,1,2,1;1,1,1,2];
>> B=[2,1,1,1,1;1,2,1,1,1;1,1,2,1,1;1,1,1,2,1];
>> [rank(A), rank(B)]

ans =

4 4

>> b = [1,1,1,1]';
```

We see that the matrices *A* and *B* (the augmented matrix) both have rank 4, which also coincides with the number of unknowns. Thus the system has a unique solution. To calculate the solution we can use any of the commands shown below.

```
>> x = nnls(A,b)

x =

0.2000
0.2000
0.2000
0.2000
```

```
>> x = bicg(A,b)
bicg converged at iteration 1 to a solution with relative residual 0

x =

0.2000
0.2000
0.2000
0.2000

>> x = bicgstab(A,b)
bicgstab converged at iteration 0.5 to a solution with relative residual 0

x =

0.2000
0.2000
0.2000
0.2000

>> x = pcg(A,b)
pcg converged at iteration 1 to a solution with relative residual 0

x =

0.2000
0.2000
0.2000
0.2000

>> gmres(A,b)
gmres converged at iteration 1 to a solution with relative residual 0

ans =

0.2000
0.2000
0.2000
0.2000

>> x = lsqr(A,b)
lsqr converged at iteration 2 to a solution with relative residual 0

x =

0.2000
0.2000
0.2000
0.2000
```

```
>> A\b'

ans =

0.2000
0.2000
0.2000
0.2000
```

CHAPTER 5

■ ■ ■

Matrices, Vector Spaces and Linear Applications

Matrix Notation

We have already seen how vectors and matrices are represented in MATLAB in the chapter dedicated to variables, however we shall recall here the notation.

Consider the matrix

$$A = \left(A_{ij}\right) = \begin{pmatrix} a_{11} & a_{12} & a_{13} & \cdots & a_{1n} \\ a_{21} & a_{22} & a_{23} & \cdots & a_{2n} \\ \cdots & \cdots & \cdots & \cdots & \cdots \\ a_{m1} & a_{m2} & a_{m3} & \cdots & a_{mm} \end{pmatrix}, i = 1,2,3,\cdots,m \; j = 1,2,3,\cdots,n.$$

You can enter this in MATLAB in the following ways:

```
A = [a11,a12,...,a1n ; a21,a22,...,a2n ; ... ; am1,am2,...,amn]
```

```
A = [a11 a12 ... a1n ; a21 a22 ... a2n ; ... ; am1 am2 ... amn]
```

On the other hand, a vector $V = (v1, v2, ..., vn)$ is introduced as a special case of a matrix with a single row (i.e. a matrix of dimension $1 \times n$) in the following form:

```
V = [v1, v2, ..., vn]
```

```
V = [v1 v2 ... vn]
```

Matrix Operations

MATLAB includes commands that allow you to perform the most common symbolic and numerical operations with matrices. The following table shows the most important such operations.

A + B   *Sum of matrices A and B*

    >> A=[-1 7 2;i -i 8; 3 1 4]

    A =

```
    -1.0000            7.0000           2.0000
 0 + 1.0000i      0 - 1.0000i          8.0000
     3.0000            1.0000           4.0000
```

    >> B=[1 2 3; 1+i 1-2i 1-3i; -3 -5 -i]

    B =

```
         1.0000            2.0000            3.0000
 1.0000 + 1.0000i  1.0000 - 2.0000i  1.0000 - 3.0000i
        -3.0000           -5.0000        0 - 1.0000i
```

    >> A+B

    ans =

```
              0            9.0000            5.0000
 1.0000 + 2. 0000i  1.0000 - 3. 0000i  9.0000 - 3. 0000i
              0           -4.0000       4.0000 - 1. 0000i
```

A – B   *Difference of matrices A and B*

    >> A-B

    ans =

```
 -2.0000            5.0000                  -1.0000
 -1.0000           -1.0000 + 1.0000i   7.0000 + 3.0000i
  6.0000            6.0000              4.0000 + 1.0000i
```

A * B   *Product of matrices A and B*

    >> A*B

    ans =

```
     0 + 7.0000i  -5.0000 -14.0000i    4.0000 -23.0000i
        -23.0000 -42.0000 + 1.0000i   -3.0000 - 6.0000i
 -8.0000 + 1.0000i -13.0000 - 2.0000i  10.0000 - 7.0000i
```

(*continued*)

c * A	*Product of a scalar with a matrix*	

```
>> i*A

ans =

0 - 1.0000i        0 + 7.0000i        0 + 2.0000i
   -1.0000            1.0000          0 + 8.0000i
0 + 3.0000i        0 + 1.0000i        0 + 4.0000i
```

expm (A) *The matrix exponential e^A calculated via eigenvalues*

```
>> expm(A)

ans =

1.0e+003 *

0.5710 + 0.0674i   0.7081 - 0.0337i   1.7019 - 0.0338i
0.5710 + 0.0674i   0.7081 - 0.0337i   1.7018 - 0.0337i
0.5710 + 0.0675i   0.7082 - 0.0337i   1.7018 - 0.0337i
```

expm1 (A) *The matrix exponential e^A calculated via Padé approximants*

```
> expm1(A)

ans =

1.0e+003 *

-0.0006              1.0956             0.0064
-0.0005 + 0.0008i   -0.0005 - 0.0008i   2.9800
0.0191               0.0017             0.0536
```

logm (A) *The matrix Napierian logarithm of Λ*

```
>> logm(A)

ans =

 1.3756 + 0.0063i   2.4201 + 0.4906i  -1.7163 - 0.4969i
-0.9903 + 0.1445i   1.7284 - 0.2954i   1.3413 + 0.1509i
 0.6464 - 0.0412i  -0.6375 - 0.1572i   2.0705 + 0.1984i
```

(continued)

sqrtm (A)	*Square root of the square matrix A*

```
>> sqrtm(A)

ans =

 1.1538 - 0.0556i   2.4904 + 0.3474i  -0.8158 - 0.2918i
-0.6332 + 0.2331i   1.5192 - 0.3779i   1.9424 + 0.1449i
 0.8187 - 0.0083i  -0.2678 - 0.0893i   2.2775 + 0.0975i
```

funm **(A, 'function')**	*Applies the function to the square matrix A. The functions that can be used are EXP, LOG, COS, SIN, COSH, SINH, SQRTM and EXPM*

```
>> funm(A,'log')

ans =

 1.3756 +  0.0063i   2.4201 + 0.4906i  -1.7163 - 0.4969i
-0.9903 + 0.1445i   1.7284 - 0.2954i   1.3413 + 0.1509i
 0.6464 - 0.0412i   -0.6375 - 0.1572i   2.0705 + 0.1984i

>> funm(A,'sinh')

ans =

1.0e+002 *

2.8840 + 0.3729i   3.4704 - 0.1953i   8.5505 - 0.1776i
2.8821 + 0.3256i   3.5574 - 0.1265i   8.4652 - 0.1992i
2.8359 + 0.3291i   3.5556 - 0.1738i   8.5133 - 0.1553i

>> funm(A,'cos')

ans =

-22.0565 + 8.2759i    20.1371 -22.2895i    1.7740 +14.0136i
  2.0152 + 10.6436i   -22.5464 + 2.7537i   20.3857 -13.3973i
  6.7526 - 6.1638i     1.5253 + 5.1214i   -8.4234 + 1.0424i
```

transpose(A) or A'	*The transpose of the matrix A*

```
>> transpose(A)

ans =

-1.0000        0 + 1.0000i   3.0000
 7.0000        0 - 1.0000i   1.0000
 2.0000              8.0000   4.0000
```

(continued)

inv (A)	*The inverse (A⁻¹) of the square matrix A*

```
>> inv(A)

ans =

 -0.0430 - 0.0266i   -0.1465 - 0.0133i   0.3145 + 0.0400i
  0.1373 - 0.0102i   -0.0564 - 0.0051i   0.0441 + 0.0154i
 -0.0020 + 0.0225i    0.1240 + 0.0113i   0.0031 - 0.0338i

>> A*inv(A)

ans =

 1.0000 + 0.0000i            0 + 0.0000i           -0.0000
              0     1.0000 + 0.0000i   0.0000 + 0.0000i
 0.0000 + 0.0000i     0.0000 + 0.0000i           1.0000
```

det (A)	*Determinant of the square matrix A*

```
>> det(A)

ans =

1.7600e+002 -1.6000e+001i
```

rank (A)	*Rank of the matrix A*

```
>> rank(A)

ans =

⌐3
```

trace (A)	*The trace of A, i.e. the sum of the elements of the diagonal of A*

```
>> trace(A)

ans =

3.0000 - 1.0000i
```

svd (A)	*Returns the vector of singular values of A, which are the square roots of the eigenvalues of the symmetric matrix A'A.*

```
>> svd(A)

ans =

9.7269
6.6228
2.7434
```

(continued)

[U, S, V] = svd (A)	*Returns the diagonal matrix S of singular values of A (in decreasing order of magnitude) and the matrices U and V such that A = U * S * V'*

```
>> [U,S,V]=svd(A)

U =

 -0.1891 - 0.4193i  -0.6966 - 0.5354i  -0.0595 + 0.1139i
 -0.5350 - 0.5583i   0.3725 + 0.1937i  -0.4752 - 0.0029i
 -0.2989 - 0.3181i   0.2210 - 0.0543i   0.8621 - 0.1204i

S =

 9.7269        0        0
      0   6.6228        0
      0        0   2.7434

V =

 -0.1301            0.2346            0.9634
 -0.1094 - 0.3895i  -0.7321 - 0.5179i   0.1635 + 0.0735i
 -0.6018 - 0.6762i   0.3731 + 0.0396i  -0.1721 - 0.1010i
```

rcond (A)	*Returns an estimate of the reciprocal condition number of the matrix A*

```
>> rcond(A)

ans =

0.1796
```

norm (A)	*The standard or 2-norm of A (the largest singular value of the matrix A)*

```
>> norm(A)

ans =

9.7269
```

norm (A, 1)	*The 1-norm of A (the maximum column magnitude, where the column magnitude of a column is the sum of the absolute values of its elements)*

```
>> norm(A,1)

ans =

14
```

norm (A, inf)	*The infinity norm of A (the maximum row magnitude, where the row magnitude of a row is the sum of the absolute values of its elements)*

```
>> norm(A,inf)

ans =

10
```

(continued)

norm (A, 'fro')	*The Frobenius norm of A, defined by sqrt (sum (diag(A'A)))*

```
>> norm(A,'fro')

ans =

12.0830
```

cond(A) or **cond(A,2)**	*Gives the condition number of the matrix A (by default the condition number is calculated using the 2-norm, so it is the ratio of the largest to the smallest singular value of A).*
cond(A,1)	*Gives the condition number using the 1-norm.*
cond(A,inf)	*Gives the condition number using the infinity norm.*
cond(A,fro)	*Gives the condition number using the Frobenius norm.*

```
>> cond(A)

ans =

3.5456

>> cond(A,1)

ans =

5.5676

>> cond(A,inf)

ans =

5.1481

>> cond(A,'fro')

ans =

4.9266
```

Z = null (A)	*Gives an orthonormal basis for the null space of A obtained from the singular value decomposition, i.e. AZ has negligible elements, size(Z,2) is the nullity of A, and Z'Z = I.*

```
>> null([1 2 3;4 5 6;7 8 9])

ans =

-0.4082
0.8165
-0.4082
```

(continued)

Z = null (A, 'r')	*Gives a rational basis for the null space obtained from the reduced row echelon form. AZ is zero, size(Z,2) is an estimate for the nullity of A, and, if A is a small matrix with integer elements, the elements of the reduced row echelon form (as computed using rref) are ratios of small integers.*

```
>> null([1 2 3;4 5 6;7 8 9],'r')

ans =

1
-2
1
```

Q = orth(A) **(Q′Q = I).**	*Returns an orthonormal basis for the range of A. The columns of Q are vectors, which span the range of A. The number of columns in Q is equal to the rank of A.*

```
>> orth([1 2 3;4 5 6;7 8 9])

ans =

-0.2148     0.8872
-0.5206     0.2496
-0.8263    -0.3879
```

subspace (A, B)	*Finds the angle between two subspaces specified by the columns of A and B. If A and B are column vectors of unit length, this is the same as acos(abs(A′*B)).*

```
>> subspace(A,B)

ans =

1.1728e-015
```

rref (A)	*Produces the reduced row echelon form of A using Gauss-Jordan elimination with partial pivoting. The number of non-zero rows of rref (A) is the rank of A.*

```
>> rref([1 2 3;4 5 6;7 8 9])

ans =

1     0    -1
0     1     2
0     0     0
```

A ^ p	*Raises the matrix A to the power of the scalar p.*

```
>> A^3

ans =

1.0e+002 *

1.8600 - 0.1200i    1.0400 + 0.5400i    2.2200 - 0.4200i
0.6400 - 0.1000i    2.1400 - 0.2000i    2.3400 + 0.3000i
0.8200 + 0.2400i    0.9200 - 0.1800i    3.3800 - 0.0600i
```

(continued)

p ^ A   *Raises the scalar p to the power of the matrix A.*

>> 3^A

ans =

1.0e+003 *

```
1.2568 + 0.1484i    1.5585 - 0.0742i    3.7457 - 0.0742i
1.2568 + 0.1484i    1.5586 - 0.0742i    3.7456 - 0.0742i
1.2568 + 0.1485i    1.5586 - 0.0742i    3.7456 - 0.0742i
```

diag (V, k)   *Builds a diagonal square matrix of order n + |k| from the n elements of the vector V in the k-th diagonal. If k = 0 the diagonal is the main diagonal, if k > 0 the diagonal is k places above the main diagonal. If k < 0 the diagonal is k places below the main diagonal. In addition diag(V)=diag(V,0).*

>> diag([1 2 3 4 5 6])

ans =

```
1    0    0    0    0    0
0    2    0    0    0    0
0    0    3    0    0    0
0    0    0    4    0    0
0    0    0    0    5    0
0    0    0    0    0    6
```

>> diag([1 2 3 4 5 6],1)

ans =

```
0    1    0    0    0    0    0
0    0    2    0    0    0    0
0    0    0    3    0    0    0
0    0    0    0    4    0    0
0    0    0    0    0    5    0
0    0    0    0    0    0    6
0    0    0    0    0    0    0
```

>> diag([1 2 3 4 5 6],-2)

ans =

```
0    0    0    0    0    0    0    0
0    0    0    0    0    0    0    0
1    0    0    0    0    0    0    0
0    2    0    0    0    0    0    0
0    0    3    0    0    0    0    0
0    0    0    4    0    0    0    0
0    0    0    0    5    0    0    0
0    0    0    0    0    6    0    0
```

(*continued*)

triu (A, k)	*Constructs an upper triangular matrix from the elements of A that are placed above the k-th diagonal. If k = 0 the diagonal is the main diagonal, if k > 0 the diagonal is k places above the main diagonal. If k < 0 the diagonal is k places below the main diagonal. In addition triu(A)=triu(A,0).*

```
>> triu([1 2 3;4 5 6; 7 8 9],1)

ans =

0 2 3
0 0 6
0 0 0

>> triu([1 2 3;4 5 6; 7 8 9],1)

ans =

0 2 3
0 0 6
0 0 0

>> triu([1 2 3;4 5 6; 7 8 9],-1)

ans =

1 2 3
4 5 6
0 8 9
```

tril (A, k)	*Constructs a lower triangular matrix from the elements of A that are placed below the k-th diagonal. If k = 0 the diagonal is the main diagonal, if k > 0 the diagonal is k places above the main diagonal. If k < 0 the diagonal is k places below the main diagonal. In addition tril(A)=tril(A,0).*

```
>> tril([1 2 3 ;4 5 6; 7 8 9])

ans =

1    0    0
4    5    0
7    8    9

>> tril([1 2 3 ;4 5 6; 7 8 9],1)

ans =

1    2    0
4    5    6
7    8    9

>> tril([1 2 3 ;4 5 6; 7 8 9],-1)

ans =

0 0 0
4 0 0
7 8 0
```

(*continued*)

A =
sym('[f1;f2,...,fm]')

Defines the symbolic m×n matrix with rows f1 to fn where fi = [ai1, ai2,..., ain]. The operations
and functions for symbolic matrices are similar to those for numerical matrices.

```
>> A=sym('[a,a+1,a+2;a,a-1,a-2;1,2,3]')

A =

[ a, a + 1, a + 2]
[ a, a - 1, a - 2]
[ 1,     2,     3]

>> B=sym('[b,b+1,b+2;b,b-1,b-2;1,2,3]')

B =

[ b, b + 1, b + 2]
[ b, b - 1, b - 2]
[ 1,     2,     3]

>> A+B

ans =

[ a + b, a + b + 2, a + b + 4]
[ a + b, a + b - 2, a + b - 4]
[     2,         4,         6]

>> det(A)

ans =

0

>> rank(A)

ans =

2

>> trace(A)

ans =

2*a + 2

>> triu(A,2)

ans =

[ 0, 0, a + 2]
[ 0, 0,     0]
[ 0, 0,     0]
```

(*continued*)

dot (A, B)	*Scalar product of vectors A and B*
	``` >> a = [1 2 3]; b = [4 5 6];``` ``` c = dot(a,b)```
	``` c = ```
	``` 32 ```
cross (A, B)	*Vector product of vectors A and B*
	``` >> a = [1 2 3]; b = [4 5 6];``` ``` c = cross(a,b)```
	``` c = ```
	``` -3 6 -3 ```

Decomposition of Matrices. Eigenvectors and Eigenvalues

MATLAB implements commands for the majority of known matrix decompositions and enables you to work with eignevalues and eigenvectors with ease. The syntax for the most common commands is presented in the following table.

eig (A)	*Finds the eigenvalues of the square matrix A.*
	``` >> A=rand(4)```
	``` A = ```

	``` 0.8147 0.6324 0.9575 0.9572```
	``` 0.9058 0.0975 0.9649 0.4854```
	``` 0.1270 0.2785 0.1576 0.8003```
	``` 0.9134 0.5469 0.9706 0.1419```

	``` >> B=sym('[1, a, a^2;1, a, -a;0, 0, 1]')```
	``` B = ```

	``` [1, a, a^2]```
	``` [1, a, -a]```
	``` [0, 0, 1]```

	``` >> eig(A)```

(continued)

```
ans =

2.4021
-0.0346
-0.7158
-0.4400


>> eig(B)

ans =

0
1
a + 1
```

[V, D] = eig (A)   *Returns the diagonal matrix D of eigenvalues of A, and a matrix V whose columns are the corresponding eigenvectors, so that A * V = V * D.*

```
>> [V,D]=eig(A)

V =

-0.6621    -0.7149     0.1745     0.1821
-0.4819    -0.0292    -0.6291    -0.9288
-0.2766     0.6972     0.5995     0.3178
-0.5029    -0.0438    -0.4630     0.0570


D =

2.4021          0          0          0
     0    -0.0346          0          0
     0          0    -0.7158          0
     0          0          0    -0.4400


>> [V1,D1]=eig(B)

V1 =

[ -a, a^2, 1]
[  1,  -a, 1]
[  0,   1, 0]

D1 =

[ 0, 0,     0]
[ 0, 1,     0]
[ 0, 0, a + 1]
```

(continued)

eig (A, B)	*Returns a vector with the generalized eigenvalues of the square matrices A and B. The generalized eigenvalues of A and B are the roots of the polynomial in λ: det (λ * B - A).*

```
>> C=randn(4)

C =

   -0.1241    0.6715    0.4889    0.2939
    1.4897   -1.2075    1.0347   -0.7873
    1.4090    0.7172    0.7269    0.8884
    1.4172    1.6302   -0.3034   -1.1471

>> eig(A,C)

ans =

   0.6654 + 0.6533i
   0.6654 - 0.6533i
   0.0259
   0.1997
```

[V, D] = eig (A, B)	*Returns the diagonal matrix D of generalized eigenvalues of A and B and a matrix V whose columns are the corresponding eigenvectors, so that A * V = B * V * D*

```
>> [V2,D2]=eig(A,C)

V2 =

   0.2665 - 0.0340i    0.2665 + 0.0340i    1.0000    0.4002
  -0.3908 + 0.0213i   -0.3908 - 0.0213i    0.0953   -1.0000
  -0.8463 - 0.1537i   -0.8463 + 0.1537i   -0.9489   -0.1449
   0.6062 - 0.2931i    0.6062 + 0.2931i    0.0211    0.3193

D2 =

   0.6654 + 0.6533i                0          0          0
                 0   0.6654 - 0.6533i          0          0
                 0                0     0.0259          0
                 0                0          0     0.1997
```

(*continued*)

[AA, BB, Q, Z, V]
qz (A, B) =

Calculates the upper triangular matrices AA and BB and matrices Q and Z such that
Q * A * Z = Q and AA * B * Z = BB, and gives the matrix V of generalized eigenvectors of A and
B, so that A * V * diag (BB) = B * V * diag (AA).

```
>> [AA, CC, Q, Z, V] = qz (A, C)

AA =

0.6430 - 0.6312i   0.9129 - 1.0466i   1.2477 - 0.7149i  -0.1102 + 0.2576i
              0    0.9818 + 0.9639i  -0.1338 + 0.8139i   0.2874 + 0.0652i
              0                  0             0.0482             0.0822
              0                  0                  0             0.4374

CC =

0.9663             0.1979 + 0.6630i   1.5008 - 0.7681i  -0.2960 + 0.0079i
     0                      1.4756  -0.0309 + 1.0436i  -0.1974 - 0.3071i
     0                           0             1.8638             0.1951
     0                           0                  0             2.1900

Q =

0.4727 - 0.0698i   0.3875 - 0.1637i   0.1251 + 0.3290i   0.4287 - 0.5358i
0.2342 + 0.4500i   0.0410 + 0.2938i   0.5545 + 0.3640i  -0.4572 + 0.0751i
         -0.5656           -0.0713             0.6541             0.4972
          0.4410           -0.8544             0.0909             0.2594

Z =

-0.1939 - 0.1152i   0.0800 + 0.0321i   0.8930            -0.3798
 0.2939 + 0.1469i  -0.0424 - 0.0841i   0.4423             0.8292
 0.7032 + 0.1644i   0.4323 - 0.4410i   0.0188            -0.3110
-0.3690 - 0.4283i   0.7481 - 0.2067i  -0.0812             0.2673

V =

-0.2235 - 0.1328i   0.1328 + 0.2235i   1.0000 + 0.0000i  -0.4002 - 0.0000i
 0.3388 + 0.1694i  -0.1694 - 0.3388i   0.0953 - 0.0000i   1.0000 + 0.0000i
 0.8106 + 0.1894i  -0.1894 - 0.8106i  -0.9489 - 0.0000i   0.1449 + 0.0000i
-0.4253 - 0.4937i   0.4937 + 0.4253i   0.0211 - 0.0000i  -0.3193 + 0.0000i
```

(continued)

[T B] = balance (A) *Returns a similarity transformation T such that B = T\A*T, and B has, as closely as possible, approximately equal row and column norms. The matrix B is called the balanced matrix of A.*

```
>> [T,B2]=balance(A)

T =

1.0000        0        0        0
     0   1.0000        0        0
     0        0   0.5000        0
     0        0        0   1.0000


B2 =

0.8147   0.6324   0.4788   0.9572
0.9058   0.0975   0.4824   0.4854
0.2540   0.5570   0.1576   1.6006
0.9134   0.5469   0.4853   0.1419
```

balance (A) *Computes the balanced matrix B of A. This is used to approximate the eigenvalues of A when they are difficult to estimate. We have eig (A) = eig (balance (A)).*

```
>> balance(A)

ans =

0.8147   0.6324   0.4788   0.9572
0.9058   0.0975   0.4824   0.4854
0.2540   0.5570   0.1576   1.6006
0.9134   0.5469   0.4853   0.1419
```

[V,D] = cdf2rdf(V,D) *If the eigensystem [V,D]= eig(X) has complex eigenvalues appearing in complex-conjugate pairs, cdf2rdf transforms the system so D is in real diagonal form, with 2×2 real blocks along the diagonal replacing the original complex pairs. The eigenvectors are transformed so that X = V*D/V continues to hold.*

```
>> [V,D]=cdf2rdf(A,C)

V =

0.8147   0.6324   0.9575   0.9572
0.9058   0.0975   0.9649   0.4854
0.1270   0.2785   0.1576   0.8003
0.9134   0.5469   0.9706   0.1419


D =

-0.1241    0.6715    0.4889    0.2939
 1.4897   -1.2075    1.0347   -0.7873
 1.4090    0.7172    0.7269    0.8884
 1.4172    1.6302   -0.3034   -1.1471
```

(continued)

[U, T] = schur (A)   *Returns a matrix T and a unitary matrix U such that A = U * T * U' and U'* U = eye (U).*
If A is complex, T is an upper triangular matrix with the eigenvalues of A on its diagonal.
If A is real, T has the eigenvalues of A on its diagonal, and the corresponding complex
eigenvalues correspond to the 2 × 2 diagonal blocks of T.

```
>> [U,T] = schur(A)

U =

-0.6621    -0.5327     0.5206    -0.0825
-0.4819     0.1301    -0.5815    -0.6424
-0.2766     0.8273     0.4848    -0.0637
-0.5029     0.1217    -0.3947     0.7593

T =

2.4021    -0.8133    -0.6225    -0.1304
     0    -0.0346    -0.1940     0.2110
     0         0    -0.7158     0.3496
     0         0         0    -0.4400
```

schur (A)   *Returns only the matrix T of the above decomposition.*

```
>> schur(A)

ans =

2.4021    -0.8133    -0.6225    -0.1304
     0    -0.0346    -0.1940     0.2110
     0         0    -0.7158     0.3496
     0         0         0    -0.4400
```

[U, T] = rsf2csf (U, T)   *Converts the real Schur form to the complex form.*

```
>> [U1,T1] = rsf2csf(A,C)

U1 =

 0.0394 + 0.2165i   -0.8561 + 0.0945i   -0.9360    1.1092
 0.5415 + 0.2407i   -0.7067 - 0.0479i   -0.8523    0.6459
-0.1702 + 0.0337i   -0.2203 + 0.0689i   -0.1028    0.8155
 0.1937 + 0.2427i   -0.8861 + 0.0600i   -1.0560    0.3086

T1 =

-0.8576 + 0.4577i   -1.7102 + 0.4507i    0.1154 + 0.1647i    0.9728 - 0.0995i
              0    -0.8576 - 0.4577i    0.7230 + 0.1166i    0.0766 + 0.2499i
         1.4090               0           0.9535            -0.9437
         1.4172          1.6302               0            -0.9901
```

(continued)

[H, P] = hess (A)	*Returns the unitary matrix P and Hessenberg matrix H such that A = P * H * P' and P'* P = eye (size (P)).*

```
>> [P,H] = hess(A)

P =

   1.0000        0        0        0
        0  -0.7007   0.1180  -0.7036
        0  -0.0982  -0.9928  -0.0687
        0  -0.7066   0.0210   0.7073

H =

   0.8147  -1.2135  -0.8559   0.1663
  -1.2926   0.8399   1.2997   0.0668
        0   0.6987  -0.0233  -0.3394
        0        0   0.0323  -0.4196
```

[L, U] = lu (A)	*Decomposes the matrix A as the product A = L * U (an LU decomposition), where U is an upper triangular matrix and L is a permutation of a lower triangular matrix.*

```
>> [L,U] = lu(A)

L =

   0.8920  -0.3250   1.0000        0
   0.9917   1.0000        0        0
   0.1390  -0.4552   0.2567   1.0000
   1.0000        0        0        0

U =

   0.9134   0.5469   0.9706   0.1419
        0  -0.4448   0.0024   0.3447
        0        0   0.0925   0.9426
        0        0        0   0.6955
```

(continued)

[L, U, P] = lu (A)	*Returns the lower triangular matrix L, the upper triangular matrix U and the permutation matrix P such that P *A = L * U.*

```
>> [L,U,P] = lu(A)

L =

1.0000        0        0        0
0.9917   1.0000        0        0
0.8920  -0.3250   1.0000        0
0.1390  -0.4552   0.2567   1.0000

U =

0.9134   0.5469   0.9706   0.1419
     0  -0.4448   0.0024   0.3447
     0        0   0.0925   0.9426
     0        0        0   0.6955

P =

0   0   0   1
0   1   0   0
1   0   0   0
0   0   1   0
```

R = chol (A)	*Returns the upper triangular matrix R such that R'* R =A (a Cholesky decomposition), where A is positive. If A is not positive, an error is returned.*
[Q, R] = qr (A)	*Returns the upper triangular matrix R of the same dimension as A, and the orthogonal matrix Q such that A = Q * R (a QR decomposition). This decomposition can be applied to non-square matrices.*

```
>> [Q,R] = qr(A)

Q =

0.5332   0.4892   0.6519  -0.2267
0.5928  -0.7162   0.1668   0.3284
0.0831   0.4507  -0.0991   0.8833
0.5978   0.2112  -0.7331  -0.2462

R =

1.5279   0.7451   1.6759   0.9494
     0   0.4805   0.0534   0.5113
     0        0   0.0580   0.5216
     0        0        0   0.6143
```

(continued)

[Q, R, E] = qr (A)	*Returns the upper triangular matrix R of the same dimension as A, the matrix permutation E and the orthogonal matrix Q such that A * E = Q * R.*

```
>> [Q,R,E] = qr(A)

Q =

  0.5707    0.4307    0.2564   -0.6504
  0.5751   -0.0867   -0.8029    0.1308
  0.0939    0.7694    0.0861    0.6259
  0.5785   -0.4636    0.5313    0.4100


R =

  1.6777    0.9827    0.7595    1.5263
       0    0.9201    0.2246   -0.0534
       0         0    0.3983   -0.0222
       0         0         0    0.0425


E =

  0    0    0    1
  0    0    1    0
  1    0    0    0
  0    1    0    0
```

jordan (A) **[V, J] = jordan (A)**	*Returns the canonical Jordan matrix J of the matrix A (J has the eigenvalues of A as its diagonal).* *Returns the Jordan matrix J of the matrix A and the step matrix V whose columns are the eigenvectors of A such that V⁻¹ *A * V = J.*

Here the subtitle math is $V^{-1} *A * V = J$.

```
>> jordan(A)

ans =

  -0.0346 + 0.0000i                  0                  0                  0
                 0    2.4021 - 0.0000i                  0                  0
                 0                  0   -0.4400 + 0.0000i                  0
                 0                  0                  0   -0.7158 - 0.0000i

>> [V, J] = jordan (A)

V =

   16.3153 + 0.0000i    1.3164 + 0.0000i    3.1933 + 0.0000i   -0.3768 - 0.0000i
    0.6653 + 0.0000i    0.9583 + 0.0000i  -16.2888 - 0.0000i    1.3588 + 0.0000i
  -15.9101 - 0.0000i    0.5499 - 0.0000i    5.5734 - 0.0000i   -1.2947 - 0.0000i
             1.0000             1.0000             1.0000             1.0000

J =

  -0.0346 + 0.0000i                  0                  0                  0
                 0    2.4021 - 0.0000i                  0                  0
                 0                  0   -0.4400 + 0.0000i                  0
                 0                  0                  0   -0.7158 - 0.0000i
```

(*continued*)

condeig (A)	*Returns a vector of condition numbers for the eigenvalues of A.*

```
>> condeig(A)

ans =

1.0733
1.1338
1.7360
1.6539
```

[V,D,s] = condeig(A)	*Equivalent to [V,D]=eig(A) and s=condeig(A).*

```
>> [V,D,s]=condeig(A)

V =

-0.6621    -0.7149     0.1745     0.1821
-0.4819    -0.0292    -0.6291    -0.9288
-0.2766     0.6972     0.5995     0.3178
-0.5029    -0.0438    -0.4630     0.0570

D =

2.4021         0         0         0
     0   -0.0346         0         0
     0         0   -0.7158         0
     0         0         0   -0.4400

s =

1.0733
1.1338
1.7360
1.6539
```

[U,V,X,C,S]= gsvd(A,B)	*Returns unitary matrices U and V, the square matrix X and non-negative diagonal matrices C and S such that A = U * C * X', B = V * S * X' and C' * C + S'* S = I. The matrix A is m×p, B is n×p, U is m×m, V is n×n, X is p× q and q = min (n, p).*
[U,V,X,C,S]= gsvd(A,B,0)	*Same as the previous command where m or n ≥ p. U and V have at most p columns and C and S have at most p rows.*
sigma = gsvd(A,B)	*Returns the vector of generalized singular values sqrt (diag(C'*C). / diag(S'*S)).*
X = pinv (A)	*Returns the matrix X (the pseudo-inverse of A), of the same dimension as A' such that A * X * A = A and X * A * X = X, where A * X and X * A are hermitian.*

```
>> X = pinv(A)

X =

-15.2997     3.0761    14.7235     9.6445
 -0.2088    -1.8442     1.0366     1.8711
 14.5694    -1.9337   -14.6497    -9.0413
 -0.3690     0.5345     1.4378    -0.4008
```

(continued)

hess (A)	*Returns the Hessenberg matrix of A.*

```
>> hess(A)

ans =

    0.8147   -1.2135   -0.8559    0.1663
   -1.2926    0.8399    1.2997    0.0668
        0    0.6987   -0.0233   -0.3394
        0         0    0.0323   -0.4196
```

poly (A)	*Returns the characteristic polynomial of the matrix A.*

```
>> poly(A)

ans =

    1.0000   -1.2118   -2.5045   -0.8416   -0.0261
```

poly (V)	*Returns a vector whose components are the coefficients of the polynomial whose roots are the elements of the vector V.*

```
>> poly([1 2 3 4 5 6])

ans =

    1        -21        175       -735       1624      -1764        720
```

vander (C)	*Returns the Vandermonde matrix whose columns are powers of the vector C, that is, A(i,j) = C(i)^(n-j), where n = length(C).*

```
>> vander([1-1 0 6 3])

ans =

       1        1        1        1        1
       1       -1        1       -1        1
       0        0        0        0        1
    1296      216       36        6        1
      81       27        9        3        1
```

(*continued*)

eigs(A)	*Returns a vector of A's six largest magnitude eigenvalues.*
eigs(A,B)	*Solves the equation A * V = B * V * D with symmetric B.*
eigs(A,k)	*Returns a vector with the k largest magnitude eigenvalues of A.*
eigs(A,B,k)	*Returns the k largest solutions of A * V = B * V * D.*
eigs(A,k,σ)	*Returns a vector with the first k eigenvalues of A based on the ordering specified by σ , where σ may be 'lm' (larger), 'sm' (smaller), 'lr' (largest real part), 'sr' (smallest real part), 'li' (largest imaginary part) and 'si' (smallest imaginary part).*
	Gives the first k solutions to the equation k * V = B * V * D according to the ordering σ.
eigs(A,B,k, σ)	*Returns the diagonal matrix D of eigenvalues of A matrix and the matrix V whose columns are the respective eigenvectors.*

[V, D] = eigs(A,...)

```
>> [V,D] = eigs(A)

V =

  -0.6621    0.1745    0.1821   -0.7149
  -0.4819   -0.6291   -0.9288   -0.0292
  -0.2766    0.5995    0.3178    0.6972
  -0.5029   -0.4630    0.0570   -0.0438

D =

   2.4021         0         0         0
        0   -0.7158         0         0
        0         0   -0.4400         0
        0         0         0   -0.0346
```

svds(A)	*Returns the 5 largest singular values of A.*
svds(A,k)	*Returns the k largest singular values of A.*
svds(A,k,0)	*Returns the k largest singular values of A using eigs.*
[U,S,V] = svds(A,...)	*Returns a matrix U(m,k) with orthonormal columns, a diagonal matrix S(k,k) and a matrix V(n,k) with orthonormal columns such that U*S*V' is the closest rank k approximation to A.*

```
>> [U,S,V] = svds(A)

U =

  -0.6380    0.3590    0.2155    0.6462
  -0.5202   -0.2451   -0.8111   -0.1069
  -0.2287    0.7358    0.0083   -0.6373
  -0.5197   -0.5193    0.5436   -0.4059

S =

   2.6201         0         0         0
        0    0.8590         0         0
        0         0    0.3796         0
        0         0         0    0.0306

V =

  -0.5705   -0.3613   -0.1621   -0.7196
  -0.3061    0.1444    0.9401   -0.0416
  -0.6310   -0.3268   -0.1247    0.6924
  -0.4274    0.8613   -0.2729   -0.0321
```

(*continued*)

H = hadamard (n)	*Returns a matrix with values 1 or - 1 such that H'* H = n * eye (n).*	

```
>> H=hadamard(4)

H =

1     1     1     1
1    -1     1    -1
1     1    -1    -1
1    -1    -1     1
```

hankel (V)

Returns a matrix whose first column is the vector V and whose elements are zero below the first antidiagonal. The matrix hankel(C,R) has C as its first column vector and R as its last row vector.

```
>> hankel([1 2 3 4 5])

ans =

1     2     3     4     5
2     3     4     5     0
3     4     5     0     0
4     5     0     0     0
5     0     0     0     0
```

hilb (n)

Returns the Hilbert matrix of order n, so that Aij = 1 /(i+j-1)

```
>> hilb(4)

ans =

1.0000    0.5000    0.3333    0.2500
0.5000    0.3333    0.2500    0.2000
0.3333    0.2500    0.2000    0.1667
0.2500    0.2000    0.1667    0.1429
```

invhilb (n)

Returns the inverse of the n-th order Hilbert matrix.

```
>> invhilb(4)

ans =

   16      -120       240      -140
 -120      1200     -2700      1680
  240     -2700      6480     -4200
 -140      1680     -4200      2800
```

magic (n)

Returns a magic square of order n. Its elements are integers from 1 to n^2 with equal sums of rows and columns.

```
>> magic(4)

ans =

16     2     3    13
 5    11    10     8
 9     7     6    12
 4    14    15     1
```

(continued)

pascal (n)   *Returns the Pascal matrix of order n (symmetric, positive definite and based on the Pascal triangle).*

```
>> pascal(4)

ans =

    1    1    1    1
    1    2    3    4
    1    3    6   10
    1    4   10   20
```

rosser   *Returns the 8 × 8 matrix (the Rosser matrix) which is used to evaluate eigenvalue problems. The Rosser matrix has a double eigenvalue, three nearly equal eigenvalues, dominant eigenvalues of opposite sign, a zero eigenvalue and a small non-zero eigenvalue.*

```
>> rosser

ans =

   611    196   -192    407     -8    -52    -49     29
   196    899    113   -192    -71    -43     -8    -44
  -192    113    899    196     61     49      8     52
   407   -192    196    611      8     44     59    -23
    -8    -71     61      8    411   -599    208    208
   -52    -43     49     44   -599    411    208    208
   -49     -8      8     59    208    208     99   -911
    29    -44     52    -23    208    208   -911     99
```

toeplitz (C, R)   *Returns the Toeplitz matrix (non-symmetric with the vector C as its first column and the vector R as its first row).*

```
>> toeplitz([1 2 3 4 ],[1 6 7 8])

ans =

    1    6    7    8
    2    1    6    7
    3    2    1    6
    4    3    2    1
```

wilkinson (n)   *Returns the order n Wilkinson matrix (symmetric tridiagonal with pairs of eigenvalues close but not the same).*

```
>> wilkinson(5)

ans =

    2    1    0    0    0
    1    1    1    0    0
    0    1    0    1    0
    0    0    1    1    1
    0    0    0    1    2
```

(continued)

compan (P)   *Returns the companion matrix of the polynomial with coefficients P.*

```
>> compan([1 2 3 4 5])

ans =

   -2    -3    -4    -5
    1     0     0     0
    0     1     0     0
    0     0     1     0
```

Vector Spaces, Linear Applications and Quadratic Forms

The matrix commands presented above enable you to work with vector spaces, linear applications and quadratic forms. Using these commands one can determine dependence and linear dependence of sets of vectors, change bases and work in general in two and three-dimensional vector geometry. We illustrate these applications in the following examples.

As a first example we determine whether the vectors $\{\{1,2, - 3, 4\}, \{3, - 1, 2, 1\}, \{1,-5.8, - 7\}, \{2,3,1,-1\}\}$ are linearly independent.

```
>> A = [1,2,-3,4;3,-1,2,1;1,-5,8,-7;2,3,1,-1]

A =

    1    2   -3   -4
    3   -1    2    1
    1   -5    8   -7
    2    3    1   -1

>> det (A)

ans =

    0
```

As the determinant of the matrix having the vectors as rows is zero, the vectors are linearly independent.

As a second example, we determine if the set of three vectors of R^4 $\{\{1,2,2,1\},\{3,4,4,3\},\{1,0,0,1\}\}$ are linearly independent.

```
>> B = [1,2,2,1;3,4,4,3;1,0,0,1]

B =

    1  2  2  1
    3  4  4  3
    1  0  0  1

>> rank (B)

ans =

    2
```

Since we have three vectors in R^4, they would be linearly independent if the rank of the matrix having these vectors as rows was 3. However, since this rank is 2, the vectors are linearly dependent.

As a third example we find the dimension and a basis of the linear subspace generated by the vectors {{2,3,4,-1,1},{3,4,7,-2,-1},{1,3,-1,1,8},{0,5,5,-1,4}}.

To find the dimension of the linear space we calculate the rank of the matrix formed by the vectors that generate it. That rank will be the required dimension.

```
>> A = [2,3,4,-1,1;3,4,7,-2,-1;1,3,-1,1,8;0,5,5,-1,4]

A =

    2    3    4   -1    1
    3    4    7   -2   -1
    1    3   -1    1    8
    0    5    5   -1    4

>> rank (A)

ans =

    3
```

Thus the dimension of the linear space is 3, and a basis will be formed by the row vectors corresponding to any non-singular minor of order 3 of the matrix A.

```
>> det([3 4 7; 1 3 -1;0 5 5])

ans =

    75
```

Thus a basis will be formed by the vectors {{3,4,7,-2,-1}, {1,3, - 1, 1, 8}, {0,5,5,-1,4}}.

As a fourth example will check if the vectors {{2.3, - 1}, {0,0,1}, {2,1,0}} form a basis in R^3 and find the components of the vector {3,5,1} in terms of this basis.

Given that these are three vectors in three-dimensional space, a sufficient condition for them to form a basis in R^3 is that the determinant of the matrix having these vectors as rows is non-zero.

```
>> det([2,3,-1;0,0,1;2,1,0])

ans =

    4
```

The vectors form a basis. To find the components of the vector {3,5,1} in terms of this basis, we do the following:

```
>> inv([2,0,2;3,0,1;-1,1,0]) * [3,5,1]'

ans =

    1.7500
    2.7500
   -0.2500
```

In our fifth example we consider the the bases of R³ defined as B = {{1,0,0}, {- 1, 1, 0}, {0,1, - 1}} and B1 = {{1,0, - 1}, {2,1,0}, {- 1, 1, 1}}, find the change of basis matrix of B into B1, and calculate the components of the B-basis vector {2,1,3} in base B1.

The operations to be carried out are as follows:

```
>> B = [1,0,0;-1,1,0;0,1,-1]

B =

    1    0    0
   -1    1    0
    1   -0   -1

>> B1 = [1, 0, -1; 2, 1, 0; -1, 1, 1]

B1 =

    1 0 -1
    2 1  0
   -1 1  1

>> A = inv(B1') * B'

A =

   -0.5000   1.5000   2.5000
    0.5000  -0.5000  -0.5000
   -0.5000   1.5000   1.5000
```

To find the components of the base-B vector {2,1,3} in base-B1using the change of basis matrix A, we perform the following operation:

```
>> inv(B1') * B'* [2,1,3]'

ans =

    8
   -1
    5
```

For our sixth example we find the scalar triple product of the vectors {{1,1,2},{0,1,0},{0,1,1}} and calculate the area of the triangle whose vertices have coordinates the points (0,0), (5,1) and (3,7).

```
>> dot ([1,1,2], cross ([0,1,0], [0,1,1]))

ans =

    1

>> (1/2) * det ([0,0,1;5,1,1;3,7,1])

ans =

    16
```

As our seventh example we consider a linear transformation of R^5 to R^3 whose matrix with respect to the canonical bases is as follows:

$$\begin{pmatrix} 0 & -3 & -1 & -3 & -1 \\ -3 & 3 & -3 & 3 & -1 \\ 2 & 2 & -1 & 1 & 2 \end{pmatrix}$$

We find a basis for its kernel (and hence its dimension) and find the image of the vectors {4,2,0,0,-6} and {1.2, - 1, - 2, 3}. We also find a basis for the image of the transformation.

```
>> A = [0,-3,-1,-3,-1;-3,3,-3,-3,-1;2,2,-1,1,2]

A =

    0    -3    -1    -3    -1
   -3     3    -3    -3    -1
    2     2    -1     1     2

>> null(A)

ans =

   -0.5397 -  0.1251
   -0.2787 -  0.2942
   -0.0266 -  0.6948
    0.0230    0.6021
    0.7936 -  0.2292
```

These two column vectors form a basis for the null space of A. Thus the kernel of the transformation has dimension 2. Two previous output vectors form the core of the nucleus and therefore the dimension of the kernel is 2.

To find the image of any column vector v via the linear transformation we simply compute $A*v$.

```
>> A*[4 2 0 0 -6]'

ans =

     0
     0
     0

>> A*[1 2 -1 -2 3]'

ans =

    -2
     9
    11
```

The dimension of the image of the linear transformation is equal to the rank of A.

```
>> rank (A)
```

```
ans =
```

    3

Thus the dimension of the image of the transformation is 3, and a basis of the image will be given by any three linearly independent columns of A.

```
>> det([0 -3 -2;-3 3 2;-1 -3 -1])
```

```
ans =
```

    -9

Therefore, the vectors $\{\{0 - 3 - 2\};\{-3\ 3\ 2\};\{-1\ -3\ -1\}\}$ form a basis of the image.

As an eighth example we consider the linear transformation f between two vector subspaces U and V of real three-dimensional space, such that $f(a, b, c) = (a + b, b + c, a + c)$, for (a, b, c) in U. We find the matrices corresponding to the transformations f, f^5, and e^f.

To find the matrix of f, we find the images of the canonical basis vectors under f:

```
>> f
```

```
f =
```

```
[a + b, b + c, a + c]
```

```
>> subs(f,{a,b,c},{1,0,0})
```

```
ans =
```

    1   0   1

```
>> subs(f,{a,b,c},{0,1,0})
```

```
ans =
```

    1   1   0

```
>> subs(f,{a,b,c},{0,0,1})
```

```
ans =
```

    0   1   1

The matrix A associated with the linear transformation f will then have as columns the images of the basis vectors found above. Thus:

$$A = \begin{pmatrix} 1 & 1 & 0 \\ 0 & 1 & 1 \\ 1 & 0 & 1 \end{pmatrix}$$

The matrix associated to f^5 will be A^5 and the matrix associated to e^f will be e^A.

```
>> A = ([1 0 1;1 1 0;0 1 1])'

A =

     1     1     0
     0     1     1
     1     0     1

>> A ^ 5

ans =

    11    10    11
    11    11    10
    10    11    11

>> expm(A)

ans =

    3.1751 2.8321 1.3819
    1.3819 3.1751 2.8321
    2.8321 1.3819 3.1751
```

For our ninth example we classify the bilinear form f:U×V→R and the quadratic form g:U→R defined as follows:

$$f[(a,b,c),(d,e,f)] = (a,b,c)\begin{pmatrix} 1 & -2 & 0 \\ 0 & 0 & 4 \\ -1 & 0 & 3 \end{pmatrix}\begin{pmatrix} d \\ e \\ f \end{pmatrix}$$

$$g(a,b,c) = (a,b,c)\begin{pmatrix} 1 & -1 & 3 \\ -1 & 1 & -3/2 \\ 3 & -3/2 & 4 \end{pmatrix}\begin{pmatrix} a \\ b \\ c \end{pmatrix}$$

```
>> A = [1, - 2, 0; 0, 0, 4; - 1, 0, - 3]

A =

     1    -2    -0
     0     0     4
    -1     0    -3
```

>> det (A)

ans =

    8

As the determinant of the matrix of *f* is non-zero, the bilinear form is regular non-degenerate.

>> B = [1, - 1, 3; - 1, 1, - 3/2; 3, - 3/2, 4]

B =
    1.0000 -1.0000   3,0000
   -1.0000   1.0000 -1.5000
    3,0000 -1.5000   4.0000

To classify the quadratic form, we calculate its diagonal determinants.

>> det (B)

ans =

   -2.2500

>> det([1,-1;-1,1])

ans =

    0

It turns out that the quadratic form is negative semi-definite.
We can also obtain the classification via the eigenvalues of the matrix of the quadratic form.
A quadratic form is defined to be *positive* if and only if all its eigenvalues are strictly positive. A quadratic form is defined to be *negative* if and only if all its eigenvalues are strictly negative.
A quadratic form is *positive semi-definite* if and only if all its eigenvalues are non-negative. A quadratic form is *negative semi-definite* if and only if all its eigenvalues are non-positive.
A quadratic form is *indefinite* if there are both positive and negative eigenvalues.

>> eig (B)

ans =

   -0.8569
    0.4071
    6.4498

There are positive and negative eigenvalues, so the quadratic form is indefinite.

EXERCISE 5-1

Consider the following matrix:

$$M = \begin{pmatrix} 1/3 & 1/4 & 1/5 \\ 1/4 & 1/5 & 1/6 \\ 1/5 & 1/6 & 1/7 \end{pmatrix}$$

Find its transpose, its inverse, its determinant, its rank, its trace, its singular values, its condition number, its norm, M^3, e^M, log (M) and sqrt (M).

```
>> M = [1/3.1/4.1/5; 1/4.1/5.1/6; 1/5.1/6.1/7]

M =

    0.3333 0.2500 0.2000
    0.2500 0.2000 0.1667
    0.2000 0.1667 0.1429

>> transpose = M'

transpose =

    0.3333 0.2500 0.2000
    0.2500 0.2000 0.1667
    0.2000 0.1667 0.1429

>> inverse = inv (M)

inverse =

  1. 0e + 003 *

    0.3000  -0.9000  0.6300
   -0.9000   2.8800 -2.1000
    0.6300  -2.1000  1.5750
```

To verify that this is indeed the inverse, we multiply it by *M* to obtain the identity matrix of order 3:

```
>> M * inv (M)

ans =

    1.0000 0.0000 0.0000
    0.0000 1.0000 0.0000
    0.0000 0.0000 1.0000
```

```
>> determinant = det (M)

determinant =

  2. 6455e-006

>> rank = rank (M)

rank =

    3

>> trace = trace (M)

trace =

    0.6762

>> vsingular = svd (M)

vsingular =

    0.6571
    0.0189
    0.0002

>> condition = cond(M)

condition =

  3. 0886e + 003
```

For the calculation of the norm, we find the standard norm, the 1-norm, the infinity norm and the Frobenius norm:

```
>> norm (M)

ans =

    0.6571

>> norm(M,1)

ans =

    0.7833

>> norm(M,inf)

ans =

    0.7833
```

```
>> norm(M,'fro')

ans =

    0.6573

>> M ^ 3

ans =

    0.1403 0.1096 0.0901
    0.1096 0.0856 0.0704
    0.0901 0.0704 0.0578

>> logm (M)

ans =

   -2.4766    2.2200    0.5021
    2.2200   -5.6421    2.8954
    0.5021    2.8954 - 4.7240

>> sqrtm (M)

ans =

    0.4631 0.2832 0.1966
    0.2832 0.2654 0.2221
    0.1966 0.2221 0.2342
```

To calculate e_M we try the eigenvalue, Padé approximant, Taylor expansion and condition number variants:

```
>> expm (M)

ans =

    1.4679 0.3550 0.2863
    0.3550 1.2821 0.2342
    0.2863 0.2342 1.1984

>> expm1 (M)

ans =

    1.4679 0.3550 0.2863
    0.3550 1.2821 0.2342
    0.2863 0.2342 1.1984
```

```
>> expm2 (M)

ans =

    1.4679 0.3550 0.2863                    .
    0.3550 1.2821 0.2342
    0.2863 0.2342 1.1984

>> expm3 (M)

ans =

    1.4679 0.3550 0.2863
    0.3550 1.2821 0.2342
    0.2863 0.2342 1.1984
```

As we see, all methods yield the same exponential matrix.

EXERCISE 5-2

Consider the following matrix:

$$M = \begin{pmatrix} 1/3 & 1/4 & 1/5 \\ 1/4 & 1/5 & 1/6 \\ 1/5 & 1/6 & 1/7 \end{pmatrix}$$

Find its transpose, its inverse, its determinant, its rank, its trace, its singular values, M^3, log (M) and sqrt (M).

```
>> M = sym ('[1/3.1/4.1/5; 1/4.1/5.1/6; 1/5.1/6.1/7]')

M =

[1/3, 1/4, 1/5]
[1/4, 1/5, 1/6]
[1/5, 1/6, 1/7]

>> transpose = M'

transpose =

[1/3, 1/4, 1/5]
[1/4, 1/5, 1/6]
[1/5, 1/6, 1/7]
```

```
>> inverse = inv (M)

inverse =

[300, - 900, 630]
[- 900, 2880 - 2100]
[630, - 2100, 1575]

>> determinant = det (M)

determinant =

1/378000

>> rank = rank (M)

rank =

3

>> trace = trace (M)

trace =

71/105

>> vsingular = svd (M)

vsingular =

 (12703/88200 - (1045602865/351298031616 + (102103 ^(1/2) * i) / 49787136) ^(1/3)/2 - 1030177
/ (99574272 * (1045602865/351298031616 + (102103 ^(1/2) * i) / 49787136) ^(1/3))-(3-^(1/2) *
(1030177 / (49787136 * (1045602865/351298031616 + (102103 ^(1/2) * i) / 49787136) ^(1/3))-
((102103 ^(1/2) * i) / 49787136 + 1045602865/351298031616) ^(1/3)) * i) / 2) ^(1/2)
 (12703/88200 - (1045602865/351298031616 + (102103 ^(1/2) * i). / 49787136) ^(1/3)/2 - 1030177
/ (99574272 * (1045602865/351298031616 + (102103 ^(1/2) * i) / 49787136) ^(1/3)) + (3 ^(1/2)
* (1030177 / (49787136 * (1045602865/351298031616 + (102103 ^(1/2) * i) / 49787136) ^(1/3))-
((102103 ^(1/2) * i) / 49787136 + 1045602865/351298031616) ^(1/3)) * i) / 2) ^(1/2)
(1030177 / (49787136 * (1045602865/351298031616 + (102103 ^(1/2) * i) / 49787136) ^(1/3)) +
(1045602865/351298031616 + (102103 ^(1/2) * i) / 49787136) ^(1/3) + 12703/88200) ^(1/2)

>> M ^ 3


ans =

[10603/75600, 1227/11200 26477/294000]
[1227/11200, 10783/126000, 74461/1058400]
[26477/294000, 7446  1/1058400, 8927/154350]
```

```
>> log (M)

ans =

[-log (3),-log (4),-log (5)]
[-log (4),-log (5),-log (6)]
[-log (5),-log (6),-log (7)]

>> sqrt (M)

ans =

[3 ^(1/2)/3, 1/2, 5 ^(1/2)/5]
[^(1/2)/5 1/2, 5, 6 ^(1/2)/6]
[5 ^(1/2)/5, ^(1/2)/6 6, 7 ^(1/2)/7]
```

EXERCISE 5-3

Consider the following symbolic matrix:

$$A = \begin{bmatrix} a & b & c \\ 3c & a-3c & b \\ 3b & -3b+3c & a-3c \end{bmatrix}$$

Calculate A', A^{-1}, determinant (A), trace (A), rank (A), inv (A) and A^2.

>> A = sym('[a,b,c; 3*c,a-3*c,b; 3*b,-3*b+3*c,a-3*c]')

```
A =

[    a,        b,        c]
[3 * c, a - 3 * c, b]
[3 * b, 3 * c - 3 * b - 3 * c]
```

>> transpose (A)

```
ans =

[a, 3 * c, 3 * b]
[(b) - 3 * c, 3 * c - 3 * b]
[c, b, a - 3 * c]
```

>> **pretty (det (A))**

```
  3       2         2              2       3       2       3
 a - 6 a c + 3 a b - 9a b c + 9 a c + 3 b + 9 b c + 9 c
```

>> **pretty (trace (A))**

```
 3 a - 6 c
```

>> **rank (A)**

ans =

3

>> **simplify(inv(A))**

ans =

```
[ (a^2 - 6*a*c + 3*b^2 - 3*b*c + 9*c^2)/(c^2*(9*a + 9*b) - c*(6*a^2 + 9*b*a) + 3*a*b^2 + a^3
+ 3*b^3 + 9*c^3),          -(a*b - 3*c^2)/(c^2*(9*a + 9*b) - c*(6*a^2 + 9*b*a) + 3*a*b^2 +
a^3 + 3*b^3 + 9*c^3),    (b^2 + 3*c^2 - a*c)/(c^2*(9*a + 9*b) - c*(6*a^2 + 9*b*a) + 3*a*b^2 +
a^3 + 3*b^3 + 9*c^3)]
[             (3*b^2 + 9*c^2 - 3*a*c)/(c^2*(9*a + 9*b) - c*(6*a^2 + 9*b*a) + 3*a*b^2 + a^3
+ 3*b^3 + 9*c^3), -(c*(3*a + 3*b) - a^2)/(9*b*c^2 - 6*a^2*c + a*(3*b^2 - 9*b*c + 9*c^2) +
a^3 + 3*b^3 + 9*c^3),        -(a*b - 3*c^2)/(c^2*(9*a + 9*b) - c*(6*a^2 + 9*b*a) + 3*a*b^2 +
a^3 + 3*b^3 + 9*c^3)]
[               -(3*a*b - 9*c^2)/(c^2*(9*a + 9*b) - c*(6*a^2 + 9*b*a) + 3*a*b^2 + a^3
+ 3*b^3 + 9*c^3), (3*b^2 + 3*a*b - 3*a*c)/(c^2*(9*a + 9*b) - c*(6*a^2 + 9*b*a) + 3*a*b^2 +
a^3 + 3*b^3 + 9*c^3), -(c*(3*a + 3*b) - a^2)/(9*b*c^2 - 6*a^2*c + a*(3*b^2 - 9*b*c + 9*c^2) +
a^3 + 3*b^3 + 9*c^3)]
```

>> **pretty(simplify(A^2))**

```
+-                                                                         -+
|        2                      2                        2     2            |
|      a  + 6 b c,        3 c  - 6 b c + 2 a b,        b  - 3 c  + 2 a c     |
|                                                                          |
|      2     2                    2            2                       2    |
|   3 b  - 9 c  + 6 a c,     6 b c - 3 b  + (a - 3 c) ,    2 b (a - 3 c) + 3 c     |
|                                                                          |
|      2              2                                           2     2   |
|   9 c  - 18 b c + 6 a b, 3 b  - 2 (a - 3 c) (3 b - 3 c), 6 b c - 3 b  + (a - 3 c)     |
+-                                                                         -+
```

EXERCISE 5-4

Consider the following matrices A and B:

$$A = \begin{bmatrix} \cosh(a) & \sinh(a) \\ \sinh(a) & \cosh(a) \end{bmatrix} \qquad B = \begin{bmatrix} \sinh(a) & \cosh(a) \\ \cosh(a) & \sinh(a) \end{bmatrix}$$

a. Calculate $M1 = A^2 + B^2$, $M2 = A^2 - B^2$, A^n, B^n, e^A, e^B

b. Find the inverse, determinant, trace and the norms of the matrices A and B.

```
>> A = sym('[cosh(a),sinh(a);sinh(a),cosh(a)]')
```

A =

```
[ cosh(a), sinh(a)]
[ sinh(a), cosh(a)]
```

```
>> B = sym('[sinh(a),cosh(a);cosh(a),sinh(a)]')
```

B =

```
[ sinh(a), cosh(a)]
[ cosh(a), sinh(a)]
```

```
>> M1 = A^2+B^2
```

M1 =

```
[ 2*cosh(a)^2 + 2*sinh(a)^2,          4*cosh(a)*sinh(a)]
[ 4*cosh(a)*sinh(a),          2*cosh(a)^2 + 2*sinh(a)^2]
```

```
>> pretty(simplify(M1))
```

```
+-                              -+
|            2                   |
|   4 sinh(a)  + 2,   2 sinh(2 a) |
|                                |
|                    2           |
|     2 sinh(2 a),  4 sinh(a)  + 2 |
+-                              -+
```

```
>> M2 = A^2-B^2
```

M2 =
```
[ 0, 0]
[ 0, 0]
```

To calculate A^n and B^n, we first find their successive powers to try to see the general rule:

```
>> [simplify(A^2),simplify(A^3),simplify(A^4)]

ans =

[ cosh(2*a), sinh(2*a), cosh(3*a), sinh(3*a), cosh(4*a), sinh(4*a)]
[ sinh(2*a), cosh(2*a), sinh(3*a), cosh(3*a), sinh(4*a), cosh(4*a)]

>> [simplify(B^2),simplify(B^3),simplify(B^4)]

ans =

[ cosh(2*a), sinh(2*a), sinh(3*a), cosh(3*a), cosh(4*a), sinh(4*a)]
[ sinh(2*a), cosh(2*a), cosh(3*a), sinh(3*a), sinh(4*a), cosh(4*a)]
```

The form of the general rule is now evident:

$$A^n = B^n = \begin{bmatrix} \cosh(na) & \sinh(na) \\ \sinh(na) & \cosh(na) \end{bmatrix}$$

```
>> simplify(inv(A))

ans =

[  cosh(a), -sinh(a)]
[ -sinh(a),  cosh(a)]

>> simplify(inv(B))

ans =

[ -sinh(a),  cosh(a)]
[  cosh(a), -sinh(a)]

>> simplify(det(A))

ans =

1

>> simplify(det(B))

ans =

-1

>> simplify(trace(A))

ans =
```

```
2*cosh(a)

>> simplify(trace(B))

ans =

2*sinh(a)

>> simplify(exp(A))

ans =

[ exp(cosh(a)), exp(sinh(a))]
[ exp(sinh(a)), exp(cosh(a))]

>> simplify(exp(B))

ans =

[ exp(sinh(a)), exp(cosh(a))]
[ exp(cosh(a)), exp(sinh(a))]
```

EXERCISE 5-5

Consider a normally distributed random square matrix A of order 3. Calculate the diagonal matrix D with diagonal entries the eigenvalues of A and the matrix V whose columns are the coreresponding eigenvectors (if the output is complex, transform it to real form).

Find the balanced matrix of A, and real and complex forms of its Schur decomposition.

Find the coefficients of the characteristic polynomial of the matrix A.

Calculate the upper triangular matrix R of the same dimension as the matrix A, the permutation matrix E and the orthogonal matrix Q such that $A * E = Q * R$ and check the result.

Consider the Hessenberg matrix B of A and calculate the diagonal matrix D of generalized eigenvalues of A and B, and a matrix V whose columns are the corresponding eigenvectors, satisfying $A * V = B * V * D$. Also calculate the vector of generalized singular values of A and B.

```
>> A=randn(3)

A =

   -0.4326    0.2877    1.1892
   -1.6656   -1.1465   -0.0376
    0.1253    1.1909    0.3273
```

```
>> [V,D] = eig(A)

V =

   0.2827     0.4094 - 0.3992i    0.4094 + 0.3992i
   0.8191    -0.0950 + 0.5569i   -0.0950 - 0.5569i
  -0.4991              0.5948              0.5948

D =

  -1.6984                 0                        0
        0      33 + 1.0309i                        0
        0                 0          0.2233 - 1.0309i

>> [V,D] = cdf2rdf(V,D)

V =

   0.2827     0.4094    -0.3992
   0.8191    -0.0950     0.5569
  -0.4991     0.5948          0
D =

  -1.6984 0 0
        0   0.2233    1.0309
        0  -1.0309    0.2233

>> [T,B] = balance(A)

T =

    1 0 0
    0 1 0
    0 0 1

B =

  -0.4326     0.2877     1.1892
  -1.6656    -1.1465    -0.0376
   0.1253     1.1909     0.3273

>> [U, T] = schur (A)

U =

   0.2827     0.2924     0.9136
   0.8191    -0.5691    -0.0713
  -0.4991    -0.7685     0.4004
```

```
T =

   -1.6984    0.2644   - 1.2548
        0    0.2233     0.7223
        0   -1.4713     0.2233

>> [U, T] = rsf2csf (U, T)

U =

    0.2827   -0.7482 + 0.1678i    0.2395 - 0.5242i
    0.8191    0.0584 - 0.3266i   -0.4661 + 0.0409i
   -0.4991   -0.3279 - 0.4410i   -0.6294 - 0.2298i

T =

   -1.6984    1.0277 + 0.1517i    0.2165 + 0.7201i
        0    0.2233 + 1.0309i    0.7490 - 0.0000i
        0                   0    0.2233 - 1.0309i

>> poly(A)

ans =

    1.0000    1.2517    0.3540    1.8895
```

Next we calculate the upper triangular matrix *R* of the same dimension as the matrix *A* of the above example, the permutation matrix *E* and the orthogonal matrix *Q* such that $A * E = Q * R$ and check the result.

```
>> [Q, R, E] = qr (A)

Q =

   -0.2507    0.4556   -0.8542
   -0.9653   -0.0514    0.2559
    0.0726    0.8887    0.4527

R =

    1.7254    1.1211   -0.2380
         0    1.2484    0.8346
         0         0   -0.8772

E =

     1 0 0
     0 1 0
     0 0 1
```

```
>> A * E

ans =

   -0.4326    0.2877    1.1892
   -1.6656   -1.1465   -0.0376
    0.1253    1.1909    0.3273

>> Q * R

ans =

   -0.4326   0.2877   1.1892
   -1.6656  -1.1465  -0.0376
    0.1253   1.1909   0.3273
```

Thus the matrices do indeed satisfy $A * E = Q * R$.

Now we consider the Hessenberg matrix B of A, we calculate the diagonal matrix D of generalized eigenvalues of A and B, and a matrix V whose columns are the corresponding eigenvectors, so that $A * V = B * V * D$. In addition we calculate the vector of generalized singular values of A and B.

```
>> B = hess (A)

B =

   -0.4326   - 0.1976    1.2074
    1.6703   - 1.2245    0.1544
         0   - 1.0741    0.4053

>> [V, D] = eig (A, B)

V =

    0.0567    1.0000    1.0000
   -0.0354  - 0.4998    0.5297
   -1.0000    0.4172    0.3785

D =

    1.0000         0         0
         0   - 0.4722         0
         0         0   - 2.1176

>> A * V

ans =

   -1.2245   - 0.0803    0.1699
   -0.0137   - 1.1082   - 2.2872
   -0.3649   - 0.3334    0.8801
```

```
>> B * V * D

ans =

    -1.2245 - 0.0803 0.1699
    -0.0137 - 1.1082 - 2.2872
    -0.3649 - 0.3334 0.8801

>> sigma = gsvd (A, B)

sigma =

    0.2874
    1.0000
    3.4799
```

EXERCISE 5-6

Consider the 3×3 matrix *A* below:

$$\begin{pmatrix} 1 & 5 & -2 \\ -7 & 3 & 1 \\ 2 & 2 & -2 \end{pmatrix}$$

Find the LU, QR, Cholesky, Schur, Hessenberg and singular value decompositions of *A*, checking that the results are correct. Also find the pseudoinverse of *A*.

First, we find the Schur decomposition, checking that the result is correct.

```
>> A = [1, 5, - 2; - 7, 3, 1; 2, 2, - 2];
>> [U, T] = schur (A)

U =

    -0.0530 - 0.8892 - 0.4544
    -0.9910 - 0.0093   0.1337
     0.1231 - 0.4573   0.8807

T =

    2.4475 - 5.7952 - 4.6361
    5.7628   0.3689   2.4332
    0          0      - 0.8163
```

Now we check that $U * T * U' = A$ and that $U * U' = eye(3)$:

```
>> [U * T * U', U * U']
```

ans =

```
   1.0000 5.0000 - 2.0000 1.0000 0.0000 0.0000
  -7.0000 3,0000    1.0000 0.0000 1.0000 0.0000
   2.0000 2.0000 - 2.0000 0.0000 0.0000 1.0000
```

Now we find the LU, QR, Cholesky, Hessenberg and singular value decompositions, checking the results for each case:

```
>> [L, U, P] = lu (A)
```

L =

```
   1.0000 0 0
  -0.1429 1.0000 0 lower triangular matrix
  -0.2857 0.5263 1.0000
```

U =

```
  -7.0000 3,0000 1.0000
        0 5.4286 - 1.8571 upper triangular matrix
        0 0 - 0.7368
```

P =

```
   0 1 0
   1 0 0
   0 0 1
```

```
>> [P * A, L * U]
```

ans =

```
  -7    3    1    -7    3    1
   5    1  - 2     1    5  - 2  we have P * A = L * U
   2    2   -2     2    2   -2
```

```
>> [Q, R, E] = qr (A)
```

Q =

```
  -0.1361 - 0.8785 - 0.4579
   0.9526 - 0.2430   0.1831
  -0.2722 - 0.4112   0.8700
```

R =

```
  -7.3485   1.6330   1.7691
        0 - 5.9442   2.3366    upper triangular matrix
        0        0 - 0.6410
```

```
E =

    1 0 0
    0 1 0
    0 0 1

>> [A * E, Q * R]

ans =

    1.0000 5.0000 - 2.0000 1.0000 5.0000 - 2.0000
   -7.0000 3.0000    1.0000 - 7.0000 3.0000 1.0000
    2.0000 2.0000 - 2.0000 2.0000 2.0000 - 2.0000

    Then, A * E = Q * R.

>> R = chol (A)

??? Error using == > chol
Matrix must be positive definite.
```

An error message is returned because the matrix is not positive definite.

```
>> [H, p] = hess (A)

P =

    1.0000        0      0
        0 - 0.9615 0.2747
        0   0.2747 0.9615

H =

    1.0000 - 5.3571 - 0.5494
    7.2801   1.8302 - 2.0943
        0 - 3.0943 - 0.8302

>> [P * H * P ', P' * P]

ans =

    1.0000   5.0000 - 2.0000 1.0000      0      0
   -7.0000   3,0000   1.0000      0 1.0000      0
    2.0000   2.0000 - 2.0000      0      0 1.0000
```

Then $PHP'= A$ and $P'P= I$.

```
>> [U, S, V] = svd (A)
```

U =

```
    -0.1034 - 0.8623    0.4957
    -0.9808    0.0056 - 0.1949
     0.1653 - 0.5064 - 0.8463
```

S =

```
    7.8306        0            0
        0    6.2735            0       diagonal matrix
        0        0       0.5700
```

V =

```
    0.9058 - 0.3051 0.2940
   -0.3996 - 0.8460 0.3530
   -0.1411   0.4372 0.8882
```

>> U * S * V'

ans =

```
    1.0000 5.0000 - 2.0000
   -7.0000 3,0000    1.0000           we see that USV'= A
    2.0000 2.0000 - 2.0000
```

Now we calculate the pseudoinverse of the matrix A:

>> X = pinv (A)

X =

```
    0.2857 - 0.2143 - 0.3929
    0.4286 - 0.0714 - 0.4643
    0.7143 - 0.2857 - 1.3571
```

>> [A * X * A, X * A * X]

ans =

```
    1.0000 5.0000 - 2.0000 0.2857 - 0.2143 - 0.3929
   -7.0000 3,0000    1.0000 0.4286 - 0.0714 - 0.4643
    2.0000 2.0000 - 2.0000 0.7143 - 0.2857 - 1.3571
```

Thus, we see that $AXA = A$, $XAX = X$.

EXERCISE 5-7

Consider the following matrix:

$$A = \begin{bmatrix} 1 & 0 & 0 \\ 0 & \cos(a) & -\sin(a) \\ 0 & \sin(a) & \cos(a) \end{bmatrix}$$

Calculate its eigenvalues, its characteristic polynomial, its Jordan canonical form and its singular values.

We start by defining the matrix *A* as a symbolic matrix:

```
>> A = sym ('[1 0 0; 0 cos (a) - sin (a); 0 sin (a) cos (a)]')

A =

[ 1,      0,        0]
[0, cos (a) - sin (a)]
[0, sin (a), cos (a)]

>> eigensys (A)

ans =

[                                         1]
[cos (a) + 1/2 * (- 4 * sin (a) ^ 2) ^(1/2)]
[cos (a) - 1/2 * (- 4 * sin (a) ^ 2) ^(1/2)]

>> pretty (simple (poly (A)))

                 3       2                  2
                x - 2 x cos (a) + x - x + 2 x cos (a) - 1

>> jordan (A)

ans =

[1, 0,                                            0]
[0, cos (a) + 1/2 * (- 4 * without (a) ^ 2) ^ (1/2), 0]
[0, 0, cos (a) - 1/2 * (- 4 * without (a) ^ 2) ^(1/2)]

>> simple (svd (A))

ans =

[                                                      1]
[1/2 * (4 * cos (a-comp (a)) + 2 * (- 2 + 2 * cos (2 * a-2 * conj (a))) ^(1/2)) ^(1/2)]
[1/2 * (4 * cos (a-comp (a)) - 2 * (- 2 + 2 * cos (2 * a-2 * conj (a))) ^(1/2)) ^(1/2)]
```

EXERCISE 5-8

Diagonalize the symmetric matrix whose rows are the vectors:

$$(3,-1,0),(-1,2,-1),(0,-1,3)$$

Find the similarity transform V, confirm that the eigenvalues of the original matrix are the diagonal elements of the diagonal matrix and that the diagonal matrix and the original matrix are similar.

We calculate the diagonal matrix J of A, which will consist of the eigenvalues of A on its diagonal and at the same time find the similarity transform V. To do this, we use the command $[V, J] = jordan\ (A)$:

```
>> A = [3, -1, 0; -1, 2, -1; 0, -1, 3]

A =

     3 -1  0
    -1 -2 -1
     0 -3 -1

>> [V, J] = jordan (A)

V =

     1 -1 -1
     2  0 -1
     1 -1 -1

J =

     1 0 0
     0 3 0
     0 0 4
```

We now confirm that the diagonal matrix J has the eigenvalues of A on its diagonal:

```
>> eig (A)

ans =

    1.0000
    3.0000
    4.0000
```

The matrices A and J are similar because the matrix V satisfies the relationship $V^1\ *A\ *V = J$:

```
>> inv (V) * A * V

ans =

    1.0000       0    - 0.0000
         0  3.0000         0
         0       0     4.0000
```

EXERCISE 5-9

Find a diagonal matrix similar to each of the following arrays:

$$A = \begin{bmatrix} 0 & -r & q \\ r & 0 & -p \\ -q & p & 0 \end{bmatrix}, \quad B = \begin{bmatrix} 0 & 1 & -\sin(a) \\ -1 & 0 & \cos(a) \\ -\sin(a) & \cos(a) & 0 \end{bmatrix},$$

$$C = \begin{bmatrix} \cos(a) & -\sin(a) \\ \sin(a) & \cos(a) \end{bmatrix}.$$

Diagonalize the matrices. Find the characteristic polynomial of each matrix.

```
>> A = sym('[0,-r,q;r,0,-p;-q,p,0]');
>> [V, J] = jordan (A)
```

```
V =
```

```
[(q *(-p^2-q^2-r^2) ^(1/2)) /(p^2 + q^2) - (p * r) /(p^2 + q^2),-(q *(-p^2-q^2-r^2) ^(1/2)) /
(p^2 + q^2) - (p * r) /(p^2 + q^2), p/r]
[-(p) *(-p^2-q^2-r^2) ^(1/2)) /(p^2 + q^2) - (q * r) /(p^2 + q^2), (p) *(-p^2-q^2-r^2)
^(1/2)) /(p^2 + q^2) - (q * r) /(p^2 + q^2), q/r]
[   1, 1,    1]
```

```
J =
```

```
[ -(- p^2 - q^2 - r^2)^(1/2),                            0, 0]
[                            0, (- p^2 - q^2 - r^2)^(1/2), 0]
[                            0,                            0, 0]
```

Now, we analyze the matrix *B*:

```
>> B = sym ('[0,1,-sin (a); - 1, 0, cos (a) - sin (a), cos (a), 0]')
>> J = simple (jordan (B))
```

```
J =
```

```
[0, 0, 0]
[0, 0, 0]
[0, 0, 0]
```

This shows that the matrix *B* has a single eigenvalue zero of multiplicity 3. In addition, the kernel of *B - 0 * eye (3) = B* has dimension less than three, as the determinant of *B* is zero. In particular, it has dimension one (as we see, calculating a basis with the command *null (B)* below). As the multiplicity and the dimension of the kernel differ, we conclude that the matrix *B* is not diagonalizable:

```
>> null (B)
```

ans =

```
[cos (a)]
[sin (a)]
[      1]
```

We have calculated a basis for the kernel of *B*, which is formed by a single vector, hence the dimension of the kernel of *B* is 1:

```
>> det (B)
```

ans =

0

We now analyze the matrix C:

```
>> C = sym ('[cos(a), - sin(a); sin(a), cos(a)]');
>> [V, J] = jordan (C)
```

V =

```
[1/2, 1/2]
[I/2, - I/2]
```

J =

```
[cos (a) - sin (a) * i, 0]
[0, cos (a) + sin (a) * i]
```

We now calculate the characteristic polynomial of the three matrices:

```
>> pretty (poly (A))

   3     2   2   2
  x + (p + q + r ) x
```

```
>> pretty (simple (sym (poly (B))))

   3
  x
```

```
>> pretty(simple(sym(poly(C))))

   2
  x - 2 cos (a) x + 1
```

EXERCISE 5-10

Find the eigenvalues of the Wilkinson matrix of order 8, the magic square magic(8) of order 8 and the Rosser matrix.

```
>> [eig (wilkinson (8)), eig (rosser), eig (magic (8))]

ans =

  1. 0e + 003 *

  -0.0010 -1.0200  0.2600
   0.0002  0.0000  0.0518
   0.0011  0.0001 -0.0518
   0.0017  1.0000  0.0000
   0.0026  1.0000 -0.0000 + 0. 0000i
   0.0028  1.0199 -0.0000 - 0. 0000i
   0.0042  1.0200 -0.0000 + 0. 0000i
   0.0043  1.0200 -0.0000 - 0. 0000i
```

We note that the Wilkinson matrix has pairs of eigenvalues that are close, but not equal. The Rosser matrix has a double eigenvalue, three nearly equal eigenvalues, dominant eigenvalues of the opposite sign, a zero eigenvalue and a small, non-zero eigenvalue.

EXERCISE 5-11

Consider the linear transformation f between two vector subspaces U (contained in R^3) and V (contained in R^4), such that for any point (a, b, c) in U:

$$f(a,b,c)=\begin{pmatrix} 1 & 0 & 0 \\ 0 & 0 & 0 \\ 0 & 0 & 1 \\ 0 & 0 & 0 \end{pmatrix}\begin{pmatrix} a \\ b \\ c \end{pmatrix}.$$

Find the kernel and the image of f.

```
>> A = ([1,0,0;0,0,0;0,0,1;0,0,0]);
```

The kernel is the set of vectors of U with null image:

```
>> null (A)
ans =

     0
     1
     0
```

Hence the kernel is the set of vectors {0,b, 0} with varying b. Moreover, the kernel obviously has dimension 1, since it has {0,1,0} as a basis.

```
>> rank (A)

ans =

    2
```

The dimension of the image of f must match the rank of the matrix A, which we have just seen is 2. The columns of a two column submatrix of A which has a non-singular two by two submatrix will form a basis of the image of f.

```
>> det([1,0;0,1])

ans =

    1
```

Thus a basis of the image of f is given by {{1,0,0,0},{0,0,1,0}}.

EXERCISE 5-12

Given the quadratic form $g:U{\rightarrow}R$ defined as follows

$$g(a,b,c)=(a,b,c)\begin{pmatrix} 1 & 0 & 0 \\ 0 & 2 & 2 \\ 0 & 2 & 2 \end{pmatrix}\begin{pmatrix} a \\ b \\ c \end{pmatrix}$$

classify and find its reduced equation, its rank and its signature.

To classify the quadratic form, we calculate its diagonal determinants.

```
>> G = [1,0,0;0,2,2;0,2,2]

G =

    1 0 0
    0 2 2
    0 2 2

>> det (G)

ans =

    0
```

```
>> det([1,0;0,2])
```

```
ans =
```

```
        2
```

The quadratic form is degenerate positive semidefinite.

To find the reduced equation we diagonalize the matrix.

```
>> J = jordan (G)
```

```
J =
```

```
        0 0 0
        0 1 0
        0 0 4
```

The reduced quadratic form equation is then:

$$h(x,y,z)=(x,y,z)\begin{pmatrix} 0 & 0 & 0 \\ 0 & 1 & 0 \\ 0 & 0 & 4 \end{pmatrix}\begin{pmatrix} x \\ y \\ z \end{pmatrix}=y^2+4z^2.$$

```
>> rank (J)
```

```
ans =
```

```
        2
```

The rank of the quadratic form is 2, since the rank of the matrix is 2. The signature is also 2, since the number of positive terms in the diagonal matrix is 2.

Get the eBook for only $10!

Now you can take the weightless companion with you anywhere, anytime. Your purchase of this book entitles you to 3 electronic versions for only $10.

This Apress title will prove so indispensible that you'll want to carry it with you everywhere, which is why we are offering the eBook in 3 formats for only $10 if you have already purchased the print book.

Convenient and fully searchable, the PDF version enables you to easily find and copy code—or perform examples by quickly toggling between instructions and applications. The MOBI format is ideal for your Kindle, while the ePUB can be utilized on a variety of mobile devices.

Go to www.apress.com/promo/tendollars to purchase your companion eBook.